9 Traits
of a
Life-Giving
MOM

Praise for *9 Traits of a Life-Giving Mom*

"*9 Traits of a Life Giving Mom* is a book that will stir your heart and challenge you to live a life devoted to being the mom God has called you to be. Sue knows how to get to the core issues that often overwhelm moms. With grace, encouragement, and an approachable writing style, Sue will help you find joy and peace in the high calling of motherhood. She's not afraid to tackle the tough questions every mom is struggling with in an effort to provide help and hope." *Pete Wilson, Senior Pastor of Cross Point Community Church and Bestselling Author*

"Sue Detweiler is one of the most perceptive women and gifted communicators that I know. Her voice of encouragement and words of hope in *9 Traits of a Life-Giving Mom* must be heard around the world." *Pam Vredevelt, LPC, Bestselling Author*

"Sue Detweiler is one of the most gifted and passionate Christian teachers I have ever known. Her obvious call and commitment to minister to needs of today's families is a breath of fresh air to any generation." *Pastor Brad Mathias, President Bema Media - iShine, Author "Road trip to Redemption"*

"Sue Detweiler is simply extraordinary! A gifted woman of God who serves with both grace and godly wisdom, she is a person of courage, integrity, transparency and faithfulness to the call of the Lord in her life. She sees beyond what may seem to be the impossible and goes forward in Christ realizing that HIS promise makes all things possible! The Detweiler family has become a testimony of God's love in action. Their hearts exemplify the "Spirit of Adoption," as they seek to help the lonely and discouraged to understand their full acceptance and value in Christ. Having known Sue for more than 15 years, I have developed a deep respect for her zeal for the Lord, her family, the lost and the extended Body of Christ. The Lord has called Sue to great significance and purpose." *Glenn C. Burris, President, The Foursquare Church*

"The love of God is bursting out of Sue Detweiler—out of her home, out of her heart, and out of her mouth! This daughter of the King is definitely on the move for the Kingdom. And with a divine combination of wisdom, genuine grace, and an amazingly approachable spirit...she's getting us moving with her." *Teasi Cannon, Author of "My Big Bottom Blessing: How Hating My Body Led to Loving My Life"*

"Sue Detweiler carries a message within her heart that moms need to hear. With accessible honesty and practical application, Sue provides deep truth that will transform the hearts of moms and bring life into their homes. I cannot wait to share *9 Traits of a Life-Giving Mom* with our community!" *Jessica Wolstenholm, co-author, "The Pregnancy and Baby Companion" books and co-founder of GraceforMoms.com*

"*9 Traits of a Life-Giving Mom* will help you become a better mom and leave a legacy for your children for generations to come." *Linda Barrick, author of "Miracle for Jen," Hopeoutloud.com*

To my Mom

You are a life-giving mom.
You abide intimately with the One
who gives life to all who believe.
You have cared for me in the past overlooking my own
imperfections, introducing me to the only Perfect One, Jesus.
You encourage me in the present, enjoying who I have become,
calling me to a walk of holy intimacy with the Father.
Empowered by the wind of the Holy Spirit,
you help release me into my destiny in the future
as a life-giving mom,
inspiring women in their adventure of faith.

Contents

ADDITIONAL RESOURCES

Introduction

When my four daughters were younger, I made up a cheer that we would recite at different times: "Two, four, six, eight... Who do you appreciate? Momma! Momma! She's so great!" Of course, we would cheer for different children by name. I had my own cheerleaders who gave hugs, kisses, and smiles. Back then, I actually felt like a good mom.

If we, as mothers, are not careful we can begin to find our identity in our children and their behavior. The truth is, the behavior of your children is not the measure of your value and worth as a person.

A typical book on parenting includes a step-by-step guide on how to discipline your children. Often, the underlying premise is if one adheres to the guidelines outlined in the book, the results are perfect children and a predicament-free family.

The problem is that every child has a free will. You and I can't control what our children choose. We also live in a problem-filled society where stuff just happens.

God is the only perfect Father, and He experienced something similar. He put His children in a perfect garden, and they chose to rebel. In fact, we are still dealing with Eve's choices today. She was the first mom who really had issues.

Every Mom Has Issues

Every mom since Eve has sinned against her sons and daughters. Even Mary, the mother of Jesus, lost it when she didn't know where Jesus was (Luke 2:41-50). She is the only mother who ever had a perfect son, and she was still anxious about him.

Every mom needs a safe place to talk about the real issues she is facing without feeling like she will be judged as a "bad mom." We need others to come alongside us and cheer us on as moms even when we feel like our parenting skills are lacking and we aren't going to make it through another Cheerio-filled day.

If you are picking up this book, I hope it is because you want to become the most life-giving mother you can be. If you want to realize your God-given calling as a mom, it's going to take more than a list of "dos and don'ts." It's going to take real and honest introspection into the character of your life.

Every Mom Needs Encouragement

You need to know the meaning of your life is not measured by the sum total of the mundane moments and monotonous tasks of motherhood. You need to know that what you are doing has immense purpose. You need a fresh experience of God's presence in the midst of your ordinary, hectic days.

You also need friends. Not the kind of friends who have it all together in their Instagram-perfect homes and fashion-ready children. No, you need friends who will be honest with their own struggles. Friends who will cheer you on to cross the finish line of being faithful to God within your calling of motherhood.

My daughter taught me the importance of having help on the sidelines. I ran with Rachel, helping her condition to try out for the high school soccer team. Then one night she came to me in tears.

"Mom, we have to run the mile tomorrow. It's my last chance to make the team," she said.

"What do you want me to do? Do you want me to come to practice?" I asked.

She nodded "yes" as she wiped her tears.

The next day I showed up beside the track and smiled at my daughter as she prepared to run. Then, as she came around the track for her final lap, I listened to the coach calling out the time. I knew she wasn't going to make it. I dropped my purse and sprinted across the center of the football field to the other side of the track where she was making slow progress.

I put my hand on her back and said, "YOU CAN DO IT!" Immediately, she picked up the pace and ran to the finish line with fresh energy. Everyone cheered and she made the team!

You Can Do it!

As you read *9 Traits of a Life-Giving Mom* I want you to feel the hand of God Himself on your back, running alongside you saying, "*YOU CAN DO IT! You can be the best mom in the world for your child, with My help.*"

If you are tired of being alone, let's walk down this path toward freedom together. If you have the desire to change and become all God created you to be, then I pray you will find healing and hope through my story, and the stories of other women wading through the tasks of motherhood just like you.

Welcome to a life-giving journey where it is safe for you to be honest, transparent, and real about the areas in your life that are holding you back. Let's travel together with the expectancy that God still works in the imperfect details of our lives. Let Him touch the hidden places of your heart and help you discover the joy of walking with Him. Go ahead and believe that He can take your worst and replace it with His best.

Chapter 1

BECOMING A
LIFE-GIVING MOM

"Get my baby out!" I screamed with a raspy voice. My desperate pleas for help were barely heard. Smoke filled the room as the cries of my newborn awakened me into a living nightmare. The house was on fire, and I couldn't get out.

As a young girl, my mind would wonder, "What would I do if my house caught on fire?" Then I would create a very clear, levelheaded plan. However, smoke inhalation disorients your brain.

The sounds of my precious five-week-old daughter's wails pierced my sleep. Walking to her bedroom in the dark, half-asleep, to feed her every night had never been a problem. Now, suddenly I was lost and couldn't find her doorway.

I clawed at the clothes in my closet trying to find my way out. Then, stumbling in the other direction, I felt the windowpane. It wasn't until I opened the window and looked out that I realized my house was on fire. I tried to scream for help, but no one could hear my cries.

I collapsed. In desperation, I prayed the prayer everyone prays when they think they are about to die—"*Help!*" My daughter and I would have died that night if my husband hadn't gotten home in time. Imagine his horror when he rounded the corner and could see the sky lit up by orange flames.

Cars and people filled our street, watching in horror. The home next to us, which was under construction, had already burned to the ground. A home on the other side stood engulfed in a raging inferno. The family of four stood huddled together, watching all of their belongings turn to ash.

There was only one fire truck on the scene. The other fire trucks sat motionless, waiting for a passing train. My husband grabbed the arm of the fireman. Frantically he asked, "Did you get my wife and baby out?" The fireman dropped the hose and together they ran to the front door. The neighbors had assumed we were still on vacation. They didn't realize we were trapped inside.

When I heard someone coming into our home, I began to scream hysterically, "Get my baby out!" I don't remember what the fireman who saved my life looked like that night. I just remember him holding his flashlight up and saying, "Come toward the light." I made my way toward what looked like a tiny pin-light in the smothering darkness. At last, I felt his arms as he led me out to safety.

Every Mom Needs Help

You may not have woken up to your house in flames and your child in danger, but you have needs. If you are transparent, you don't have it all together. Your life is not perfect. There may be some wonderful aspects to your life right now, but there are other areas that are just plain tough.

It's when we come to the end of ourselves that we find God. He is the source of our life. He is the maker of heaven and earth. He created you in His image. He gave you life, breath, and purpose.

If you are trying to walk through life as a mom without the help of God, you will be lonely, depressed, and overwhelmed. But if you are ready to find help, He is waiting to help you. He is ready to pour His life-giving, life-altering, life-changing power into you.

> *It's when we come to the end of ourselves that we find God.*

Think about the last time you were on a plane. Most likely you heard the flight attendant give instructions to parents with small children. "In case of emergency, put your oxygen mask on first before helping your child put on their oxygen mask." This instruction is not only helpful when on a plane, but also in life.

Every Life-Giving Mom needs to be connected to the ultimate Life-Giver. Every day you must put on your oxygen mask first before you help your children. Sure, you can pretend to have enough leftover oxygen from the day before, but you can't be a Life-Giving Mom in your own strength. Like the air that we breathe to sustain life, oxygen is a symbol for the continual supply of the breath and life of the Holy Spirit.

The Morning After the Fire

We spent a long, weary night in the hospital as the doctors examined and treated my baby and me for smoke inhalation. In the early hours of the morning we called my mom.

"Mom, we're all right." The long pause of silence was deafening. Finally, she spoke: "What happened?"

Wayne described the huge fire and how there was only one fire truck, leaving three homes devastated. The heat from the blazing inferno melted a car bumper and the shutters of our neighbors' home. People lined the street as the fire lit up the night sky. As we told Mom about the fire, her quiet peace engulfed our stress.

"You're the ones I have been praying for," she said. The month before, my mom began to meditate, fast, and pray over Isaiah 43:

> *When you pass through the waters,*
> *I will be with you;*
> *and when you pass through the rivers,*
> *they will not sweep over you.*
> **When you walk through the fire,**
> **you will not be burned;**
> **the flames will not set you ablaze.**
> Isaiah 43:2, NIV

Later I would look back on this telephone conversation and marvel at the power of prayer and the peace of my own mother. I would rejoice in how God saved us from the fire. I would celebrate—just like Shadrach, Meshach and Abednego—that God was with me in the fire. I would wonder at how the bondages of my life were burned up and I was set free. (See Daniel 3).

However, my present reality was far from tranquil. My whole life-system was on overload. *I had no home...no baby furniture...no diapers...no clothes...*

As we walked into the shell of our home trying to salvage things, my emotions were more charred than the black soot that blanketed every surface. The neighbors rallied and helped with our physical needs, but I was a mess. For the first two weeks, before the insurance company paid for an apartment, we stayed at a neighbor's house. They graciously opened their home to us while they were on vacation. It was then that Rachel, at six weeks old, began to scream uncontrollably for hours at a time. She had colic.

One day, I laid Rachel down on the blanket and slowly backed away. Her screaming drove me to the edge of feeling like I couldn't cope. I began to feel claustrophobic and trapped. My heart raced as my mind shut down. "I'm losing it," I thought. "If I don't get out of the house, I don't know what I will do." I went to the kitchen and dialed the number of a neighbor.

"Can you take my baby?" I quietly pleaded, as soon as she answered the phone. "I have to get out of here."

Hearing the tremor in my voice, the neighbor agreed to help me. No doubt, she saw my glazed look as I handed her my infant and drove off. What would have happened if she hadn't been there for me? I don't know. I was truly desperate.

Life-Giving Moms are Open to Change

Desperation is a driving force in our lives to seek change. It is during the pressure-cooker seasons in our lives when we find out our areas of weakness and vulnerability. Pressure cookers are known for being hot, dangerous, and able to blow their lid. That house fire revealed the hidden habits of my own heart that needed God's healing touch. It's the heat of life that shows the hidden fractures of our hearts.

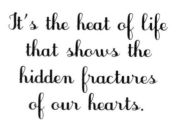

It's the heat of life that shows the hidden fractures of our hearts.

A *Life-Giving Mom uses the pressure-cooker seasons to reevaluate.* Allow your own areas of need to propel you toward getting help. As you learn new skills, you will become a better person as well as a better mom. If you have picked up this book for the first time, you will be drawn to areas you need to overcome in your own life. If you are reading this book for the second time, your season has changed and now you have another area of need.

A Life-Giving Mom is a life-long learner. Approach this journey with an open heart rather than a smug brain. Jesus said He came for the sick. It was the religious who thought they were holier than Jesus and crucified Him. They murdered the one who came to bring them life (See Matthew 27). As you begin this journey, turn off your religious notions about who you should or shouldn't be. Rather, come as you are. Shine the flashlight of God's Word into the closets of your life and look freshly at replacing the old broken habits with brand new life strategies.

A Life-Giving Mom replaces life-destroying habits with life-sustaining actions. You have the power of choice. The choices you make today will determine your destiny tomorrow. You have before you choices that bring life and choices that bring death (See Deuteronomy 30:19). Choose life.

A PRAYER TO BE A
Life-Giving Mom

You are my Life-Giver...
You are my Life-Sustainer...
You are the ONE who holds me
in Your tender arms...
As I partner with you to be a Life-Giver
to my child(ren), I trust you to lead and guide.
I trust you to fill me afresh each day
with the breath and life of your Holy Spirit.
Breathe on me fresh hope, fresh insight
and fresh wisdom.
Help me to learn your ways as I parent.
You are the best parent in the world.
I breathe in Your truth.
I breathe in Your peace.
I breathe in Your presence.
You will take me through the water and the fire,
and every difficult detail that I experience today.
I am not alone. You are with me.

Download written prayers at **www.SueDetweiler.com.**

Love

———— ✦ ————

Love is deep affection.

Love is the commitment of enduring passion.

It blooms in fond tenderness, warm intimacy,

and thrives in devoted attachment.

God is love.

He delights in all of His children.

His care and compassion never ends.

His relationship is not based on our behavior.

His love is unconditional.

He adores you and takes joy in you.

He is captivated by your uniqueness.

A Life-Giving Mom embodies God's kind of love.

She is patient and kind.

She does not demand her own way.

She doesn't keep record of wrong.

A Life-Giving Mom rejoices in truth.

She never gives up.

She never loses faith.

She is always full of hope.

She endures through every circumstance.

Her love never fails when it is anchored in the Life-Giving,

Love-Extending Power of God Himself.

Chapter 2
REPLACING MY ANGER
WITH GOD'S LOVE

As I drove to Saturday night worship, tormenting thoughts plagued my mind. *"I'm the worst mom in the world... I can't believe I blew it again... I hate my life..."*

My knuckles were white as I gripped the steering wheel. Tears streamed down my face and were reflected in the eyes of my two toddlers strapped in their car seats. Another baby girl was growing inside my belly, tucked in tight under my seatbelt.

Just hours before, my irritation had taken a sharp turn into exasperation when my daughter spilled grape juice on my newly mopped floor. Feeling overwhelmed, trapped, and exhausted, I just wanted to take a nap.

I knew I needed to get out of the house. My husband was working an extra job to help make ends meet. I was alone in the kitchen. Even though we were pastors at a local church, on Saturday nights I liked to load the girls up and visit someone else's church where I could just sit in the pews and receive.

Now, the conversation continued in my brain…*"What am I thinking? Me, trying to be a mother… God, ARE YOU THERE?"*

The last question seemed to bounce off the soiled ceiling of my car. Somehow I maneuvered into a parking space. Carrying the car seat in one hand, and squeezing too tightly the fingers of my oldest daughter with the other hand, I walked into church as a defeated mother. After signing them into childcare, I breathed a sigh of relief.

I don't think I heard the sermon that night. I just remembered communion. As my screaming tirades flashed back in my mind, I began to sob. My hands shook as I held a communion cup. The fight intensified in my mind.

You are the best mom in the world for your children.

"Who do you think you are? You hypocrite… You will never change…"

This last thought was interrupted by the pastor speaking from the pulpit: "I believe there are some of you who have believed a lie that you can't change. The truth is that Jesus' blood has paid the price for your sin, and He has delivered you out of darkness. You are free. You just need to believe it, receive it, and then act on it."

It sounded so simple. Why was I so bound? The turmoil within me began to bubble up, then calm, as though the toxic thoughts had finally been neutralized by the truth of God's Word.

A new phrase began to take shape in my mind. It was an entirely different thought. It felt like a whisper from heaven that I was finally listening to. ***"You are the best mom in the world for your children… I have called you… I will help you be a better mom… You can trust Me."***

Hope began to fill the deepest recesses of my soul. For so long I had floundered under the fog of the enemy's torment. These words were like beams of sunshine, bringing a multi-faceted rainbow of His promise: His personal promise *to me*. That night, as I took communion in faith, my life began to change.

God Will Help You to be a Better Mom

If you were to write about your most raw moment of unguarded thoughts, how would you feel? Exposed? Vulnerable? Insecure? It is our thought lives that lead to our irrational feelings. Just recounting this story from a long time ago makes me feel ashamed and a little afraid of how people will react.

Most of the time we do not talk about our thought lives. We don't want others to know about our angry outbursts. It's our instinct to keep our faults concealed. *The hidden habits of the heart can imprison our mind and emotions.*

The invisible struggle in our minds is visible to God. Our thoughts lead to choices, which lead to outward habits. Anger begins as a seed in the mind that takes root and grows. Your face begins to show your displeasure. Your body language reflects annoyance. Before you know it, your ill temper burns into rage.

Once you let the fire of exasperation linger, you have entered into the danger zone. Most crimes of passion are committed in the context of family. The battle may begin in the recesses of our minds, but it may end on the front page of the newspaper.

An emotion in itself is not good or bad, but how we choose to act upon it can be. Anger is a normal human emotion that can fuel positive things. Jesus fashioned a whip in the temple and drove out the moneychangers who were stealing from people and dishonoring God's house (See John 2:14-16). The human emotion of anger can be a righteous indignation that leads to positive change.

Most of the time, however, we become angry or frustrated when we do not get what we want. We have a goal that has been blocked or an agenda that has been thwarted. Anger that is out of control can become destructive. It can make you feel like you are at the mercy of a powerful emotion that is unpredictable and, at times, irrational.

Anger can vary in intensity from mild irritation to intense feelings of rage. Anger is accompanied by physiological changes causing your heart rate and blood pressure to go up. You also get an adrenaline rush, which acts like gasoline to fuel your "fight or flight" response.

Uncontrolled anger can be devastating to a child. Anger tears down protective boundaries of self. Anger itself can be a weapon of control and manipulation. When a parent uses anger as a weapon, the child will grow in a fear-based environment rather than a culture of love and respect.

Seeing your reflection in the mirror of God's Word brings truth of your own need to change.

Have you ever seen your own angry red face in the reflection of a mirror? I never knew I had anger issues until I was faced with the daunting task of potty-training a toddler. By the fourth mishap of the day I was pulling off her jeans with such force that I am sure it scared her. Then I screamed and caught my face reflecting back at me in the mirror: ugly, red, distorted by rage. This was the face my daughter was seeing.

Seeing your reflection in the mirror of God's Word brings truth of your own need to change. It is easy to point your finger and look at other people who battle out-of-control anger. It is another thing to honestly assess how you personally deal with anger. Whether you express, suppress, or calm your anger is your choice. Anger is not an emotion you can ignore. Unexpressed anger can come out in passive aggressive ways, such as cynical comments, cutting looks, or critical judgments, which contribute to broken relationships.

Our children can receive the brunt of our unexpressed anger. We may be angry at a situation at work and seem perfectly calm there, but then we come home and make life miserable for everyone we encounter. Children pick up on our hostility and blame themselves for it. An angry mother is the source of much pain for her children.

Learning to Walk in Love

Every Life-Giving Mom knows she needs to walk in love for her child. How do we turn our angry emotions into a life-giving force? As a mom, how can I be angry and not sin against my children? It is helpful to begin to memorize what God's Word says about anger. These verses are helpful to keep in mind.

> *"And 'don't sin by letting anger control you.'*
> *Don't let the sun go down while you are still angry,*
> *for anger gives a foothold to the devil."*
> Ephesians 4:26-27, NLT

When you or I become angry we give a foothold to the devil. When I walk in unrestrained anger I might as well open the doors to my home and say, "Devil, come on in and torture my children." The presence of evil invades our homes when we don't resolve our anger.

A practical approach I found to replace my anger with God's love was to speak God's Word out loud in moments of exasperation. I would practice when it came time to discipline our children.

Wayne and I began to facilitate family devotions when our children were small. During this time I began to teach them Scriptures that *I* needed

When you or I become angry, we give a foothold to the devil.

to meditate on and memorize. One of those Scriptures was the Fruit of the Spirit from Galatians, which says:

"But the Holy Spirit produces this kind of fruit in our lives: love, joy, peace, patience, kindness, goodness, faithfulness, gentleness, and self-control. There is no law against these things!"
Galatians 5:22-23, NLT

The times when I felt angry, I began to send our children to the designated place for discipline. I would send them ahead of me so that I could cool down. During the family devotion time we had instructed them that because we loved them we would discipline for three things: disobedience, disrespect, and dishonesty. We had them memorize these "3 D's" for discipline.

While I was cooling down, I asked my children to think about what they had done and why they needed discipline. Often, I would stand by myself saying out loud: "I have love, joy, peace, patience, kindness, goodness, faithfulness, and self-control." By the time I said this out loud, God's presence was again ruling my heart and my home.

The fruit of the Holy Spirit reveals God's divine personality and character traits, which grow over time in our human spirit. The fruit of love is one, which gives selflessly and freely. It is a good-natured love that seeks the greater good. In Scripture, the Greek word *agape* refers to a sacrificial love, the kind demonstrated by Jesus' death on the cross.

"Love is patient and kind. Love is not jealous or boastful or proud or rude. It does not demand its own way. It is not irritable, and it keeps no record of being wronged. It does not rejoice about injustice but rejoices whenever the truth wins out. Love never gives up, never loses faith, is always

hopeful, and endures through every circumstance.
Prophecy and speaking in unknown languages and special knowledge
will become useless. But love will last forever!"
1 Corinthians 13:4-8 NLT

As a mom, you have the incredible opportunity to show this agape love to your children as a fruit of the Holy Spirit at work in you and through you. His love casts out fear.

The love of a mother for a child is the strongest nurturing force on the planet. God formed the woman's body to not only bring forth life but to feed her child from her own body. This is an amazing picture of how God loves us. In Isaiah 49, God is described as a nursing mom who would never forget her children.

"Yet Jerusalem says, 'The Lord has deserted us;
the Lord has forgotten us.'
'Never! Can a mother forget her nursing child?
Can she feel no love for the child she has borne?
But even if that were possible, I would not forget you!'"
Isaiah 49:14-15, NLT

God is like a mother who can never forget her children. A mother's love makes a child feel safe and protected. Even though it is possible for an earthly mom to choose to reject her child, God will never reject you.

A Life-Giving Mom needs to model her love for her children after God's love for us. God's agape love is not selfish. It does not lash out in rage. A child feels safe in God's love. Your child is protected from hostility, bitterness, and resentment when you walk in God's kind of love.

The Path of Grace

Negative expressions of anger are not overcome by your own strength and fortitude. You must replace anger with God's love by God's grace. God is the One who called you to be a mom. He will equip you through the abundance of His grace.

We bring glory to God by becoming more like Him. You don't become a great parent in one day. You grow into greatness through God's grace.

"But grow in grace (undeserved favor, spiritual strength) and recognition and knowledge and understanding of our Lord and Savior Jesus Christ (the Messiah). To Him [be] glory (honor, majesty, and splendor) both now and to the day of eternity. Amen (so be it)!"
2 Peter 3:18, AMP

We grow in grace when we increase our knowledge of who God is. In order to understand who God is, we need to be able to see the breadth of His nature without putting Him in a box.

God is both sovereign and personal. He is holy. He is forgiving. He is a purifying fire. He is a healer. His grace is an empowering force. His presence enables you to be who He created you to be. It is by God's grace that you are able to do what He has called you to do. As a Life-Giving Mom you must know that you can only parent through God's divine enablement.

The amazing promise that God gives every mom is that His grace is sufficient. His power works best in our weakness. We have all messed up as moms. We have all blown it. Aren't you glad that your angry outbursts do not disqualify you as a mom?

With the help of God and by the grace of God, *you are able to be the best mom in the world for your children.* As your children grow and develop, you have the opportunity to grow and develop as a parent.

So look up to God right now! He is able to make you a great mom. He won't override the choices of your children, but He will give you what you need every day. So turn to Him with an expectant heart. He will replace your anger with His love.

WATCH
Watch the free video
Replacing My Anger with God's Love
at www.SueDetweiler.com.

A PRAYER FOR
Love

Loving Father,
I choose to imitate you as a dear child.
Help me to walk in your love
Even as Jesus loved me
and gave Himself for me.
Let my life be an offering to You.
Let the daily sacrifice that I make as a mom
be a sweet-smelling aroma to You.
When I am angry,
help me not to sin.
Let my lips speak words that build up my children.
Holy Spirit, be present with me
all through the day.
Help me to be kind and tender-hearted,
forgiving freely just as Jesus forgave me.
Help me grow in your grace and spiritual strength
so that I can give You glory and honor
all the days of my life.
In Jesus name I pray. Amen.
(Ephesians 4:26-5:2; 2 Peter 3:18)

Joy

❧

To be filled with Joy is to be truly alive.
Embracing life at full capacity.
Joy is contentment mingled with pleasure.
Joy is to celebrate the little things.
Joy brings strength to press forward in a grand adventure.
Joy is like an unstoppable fountain that never runs dry.
It is refreshing to everyone with newness of life.
Joy is a sunbeam that lights your path
and warms your heart.
Joy is best when shared with a friend.
Joy is the heart's celebration
of the treasures of God's goodness.
Joy is ever-present.
In God's Kingdom,
Joy will never end.
Where there is sorrow, it will cease,
but Joy comes in the morning and spreads into eternity.

Chapter 3

REPLACING MY SADNESS
WITH GOD'S JOY

―――∞∞∞―――

Within hours of receiving the phone call that my father only had weeks to live, I was on a plane heading to see him. Arriving at the hospital room, I laid my head on his chest. My quiet tears soaked his hospital gown. He patted my back and told me he loved me.

People lined the corridors of the hospital waiting to see my dad. "You are a man of great influence," I said, smiling at my father. He had influenced so many, as a businessman and an agent of change, in northern Indiana.

"Family is what matters most," he told me quietly, as several community leaders gathered in the halls waiting to see him. There was a glimpse of regret in his eyes. Regret for working so hard. Regret that he hadn't taken care of his body. Regret that the hours in his life were short.

Excusing myself, I headed to the tiny hospital chapel to pray. There was solace in God's presence. At first, I began to plead with God to do a miracle and heal my father. As I quieted myself to listen to His voice, there was a growing sense that my father was going to quickly pass from this life to the next. Sadness overcame me.

"I'm too young for this," I thought. I put my hand on the baby growing in my womb. I had left three little girls at home with my husband and friends, and here I was pregnant with my fourth daughter. The realization that my father would probably never hold my baby crept in. The weight of his loss swept over me as I wept before God.

I saw this mighty man of boldness and courage face the unknown with quiet dignity.

The three weeks that followed were both sweet and sorrowful. Our family sat in the hospital waiting room and laughed at the funny things that Dad had done through the years. We told story after story celebrating his legacy.

My father was ready to meet God. Heaven became his primary focus. We had times as a family surrounding his bed singing Christmas carols. We celebrated his birthday, as well as mine, in the hospital. I saw this mighty man of boldness and courage face the unknown with quiet dignity.

He was at home with my mom when he left his body on earth and began his journey into eternity.

I was with my mother a few hours later; we cried together and planned a ceremony that would impact the community. Senators and Amish men sat side-by-side and wept at my dad's funeral. The whole community had been changed because of his generosity and leadership.

As we traveled home as a family, sadness surrounded me. How could I go on without my dad? Who could I turn to for wise counsel?

Who would be Grandpa to my children? His loss permeated my mind and emotions.

Life Can Be Sad

Have you ever woken up and just felt down? It takes effort to get out of bed. When you look at your day, does it feel monotonous and mundane? Everything you eat is tasteless. Everything you attempt to do seems pointless. You just want to escape into a constant apathetic slumber.

Sadness is the feeling of gloom, melancholy, and the blues. Traumatic events such as a miscarriage or delivering a stillborn baby can plunge a mom into depression. You may have held your own daughter in your arms as her life drained from her body. You may struggle with a child who has autism. You may be the mom of a defiant, rebellious teenager.

Sadness is emotional pain characterized by the feeling of loss, despair, or helplessness. Sadness is considered to be a short-term lowering of your mood. Depression is when the low mood persists and becomes chronic or unceasing.

In a practical sense, sadness may be a result of any of the following:

- **Fatigue:** You may just be overly tired! Stress can cause emotional fatigue. Stressors can range from the loss of a loved one or concern for your finances, to loss of a job or worry over your child.

- **Low Serotonin:** Serotonin is a hormone in the body that impacts appetite, sleep, memory, temperature, and mood. Women dealing with depression often have low serotonin levels. Periods of stress often make it difficult to eat right or exercise, which will cause low serotonin in your body.

- **Loss, Sadness, Depression:** Along with physical factors, dwelling on negative thoughts and events can extend sadness. Constant feelings of hopelessness, anxiety, and emptiness that persist for weeks and months may be a sign of clinical depression. Seek professional help if depression continues or if suicidal thoughts occur. If these feelings prevent your normal functioning, you may be dealing with clinical depression.

It's in the seasons of difficulty that we need to remind ourselves about the greater truth. *The facts of our circumstances do not always make something true.*

FACT	TRUTH
Life can be hard.	God is always good.
Life can be painful.	God heals our pain.
Life can be disappointing.	God never disappoints.

When we experience a significant hardship, *we are tempted to believe the facts and miss God's truth.*

Just like the scars that marked Jesus after He was crucified, we have been marked by the cruel realities of our fallen world. How do we force this reality to move from our heads to our hearts? Just like the empty tomb, the power of His resurrection is available to each one of us.

> *The facts of our circumstances do not always make something true.*

What Happens When
a Mom Becomes Stuck?

What do you do before your breakthrough? What happens when you know you are stuck but don't know how to get unstuck? What happens when your feelings of sadness last for months?

A newborn baby is disorienting to everyone. You lose sleep. You lose control of your normal schedule. Your body is repairing from the trauma of birth. Some moms find it difficult to function. There may be days that you wish you could just stay in bed all day long, doing nothing.

A mom doesn't have the luxury to call in sick. I had to take care of my children whether I felt well or not. You may be a mom who once felt successful in your work environment. You gave up your job to come home. Somehow your picture of how it would be doesn't match your present reality. You may feel like you haven't accomplished anything at the end of your day. Some moms struggle with their worth and value, moving slowly on autopilot. If I peeked into your private life, right now, what would I see?

Sadness is a Part of Our Lives

It is a natural reaction for every one of us to experience sadness when a loved one dies, to suffer shock when an accident happens, or to fall into depression with the hormonal imbalances that come with giving birth. Symptoms of sorrow, trauma, and depression can resemble each other as it takes time for each one of us to heal.

Imagine the horror if you were Mary, the mother of Jesus, watching your son's slow, painful death. You could barely stand by your son on that terrible never-ending day. Hearing the sound of the whip rip out chunks of your son's flesh. Seeing the blood drip from His body as they mounted the cross on His shoulders. Smelling the scent of death in the sweat of your precious son as He carried the cross.

You can't stop them from torturing Him. You can't stop them from mocking Him. You are a mom who has no control over the outcome. You aren't strong enough to carry the cross for Him. You are powerless and can't prevent your son from dying. Mary was a mom who felt agonizing pain.

When you are at your lowest point and people around you can't truly understand the searing pain of your situation, there is One who knows your pain. There is One who can comfort you. There is One who can guide you. There is One who will not let this trial be your final chapter.

Crossing Over to the Other Side

God gives us His grace to walk through suffering and get to the other side. Jesus modeled this with His disciples. Jesus was healing both the physically sick and the inwardly tormented. The crowd began to grow by the minute. Jesus stepped into the boat with His disciples and told them to go to the other side of the lake.

"Suddenly, a fierce storm struck the lake,
with waves breaking into the boat.
But Jesus was sleeping.
The disciples went and woke him up, shouting, 'Lord, save us!
We're going to drown!'
Jesus responded, 'Why are you afraid?
You have so little faith!'
Then he got up and rebuked the wind and waves,
and suddenly there was a great calm.
The disciples were amazed. '
Who is this man?' they asked. '
Even the winds and waves obey him!'"
Matthew 8:24-27, NLT

Notice that Jesus was completely at peace and relaxed in the same storm where the disciples were horrified. Our perspective needs to shift off of the waves of our lives and onto the Words of Jesus. Jesus told them to *go to the other side*. His words carried a promise that they would and could arrive at the other side. The next time you are

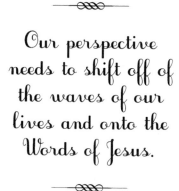

Our perspective needs to shift off of the waves of our lives and onto the Words of Jesus.

in a tough situation, focus your thoughts on what God has said.

You too can cross to the "other side" of what you are facing right now. Your perspective of hope carries you through. You can be like Jesus—sleeping peacefully, and relaxed in the storm.

When you are in the middle of a painful situation, you must believe that life will get better. We get stuck when we don't know what's coming next. Facts shout convincingly as negative thoughts bombard us. *Things will never change. I will always struggle with this. I'll never get better.*

Get Out of "Stinkin' Thinkin'"

One afternoon I admitted my negative thoughts to my own mother. She's a pretty spunky lady. She put her hand on her hip, shook her head to one side and said, *"Sue, you are in stinkin' thinkin'."*

Stinkin' thinkin' is a downward staircase leading to a dark place in our emotions. When you are stuck in this dungeon of dreary thoughts it will impact every area of your life. As a mom raising children, you can't afford to get stuck in a funk for long. Your kids will know something is wrong by the way you are irritable and hard to please. I define a FUNK like this:

F – Floundering
U – Under
N – Negative
K – Knowledge

In a FUNK your mind is spiraling out of control. One negative thought leads to the next. You may have some "knowledge" about a negative fact. *As you exaggerate the facts in your mind, they do not add up to the truth.*

Get Out of Your FUNK

You will enjoy your life to a greater degree when you reshape your thinking. God's Word is the most powerful tool you can use to change your thoughts to His thoughts. 2 Corinthians 10:3-5 gives us great insight on our thoughts:

"We are human, but we don't wage war as humans do.
We use God's mighty weapons, not worldly weapons, to knock down the
strongholds of human reasoning and to destroy false arguments.
We destroy every proud obstacle that keeps people from knowing God.
We capture their rebellious thoughts and teach them to obey Christ."
2 Corinthians 10:3-5, NLT

If you are in a FUNK, you believe a lie that makes you afraid. At the core of your problem are thoughts that you need to capture. Make your thoughts obey God's thoughts.

Every day we have the opportunity to agree with God and allow His perspective to flood us until every negative thought and emotion is forced out. It's like having a pressure washer in your mind. You have a choice to reshape your negative thoughts and replace them with a positive mindset.

Becoming pregnant with my first daughter, the intensity of hormones caught me off guard. Although I was excited about having a baby, getting bigger and bigger didn't make me a bit happy. As I packed 200 pounds onto my 5'4" frame I began to feel depressed. I had this recurring thought that would come to my mind when something went wrong: "I hate life." As I approached the end of my pregnancy, my thoughts were spoken out loud to my husband: "I hate life."

The irony of this negative thought/spoken word pattern is that it completely contradicted what God had for me. The miracle of *life* was growing inside my womb. Every time I thought or spoke "I hate life" I was directly in disagreement with God's will for my life.

The good news is that you are not alone. If you are presently in the pits, there is One who can reach down into the lowest place and bring you comfort. Like a gentle shepherd He will walk in the valley with you.

The good news is that you are not alone.

> *"The Lord is my shepherd;*
> *I shall not want.*
> *He makes me to lie down in green pastures;*
> *He leads me beside the still waters.*
> *He restores my soul;*
> *He leads me in the paths of righteousness*
> *For His name's sake.*
> *Yea, though I walk through the valley of the shadow of death,*
> *I will fear no evil;*
> *For You are with me;*
> *Your rod and Your staff, they comfort me.*

You prepare a table before me in the presence of my enemies;
You anoint my head with oil;
My cup runs over.
Surely goodness and mercy shall follow me
All the days of my life;
And I will dwell in the house of the Lord Forever."
Psalm 23, NKJV

You may not say "Yea!" when you go through a valley of despair, but you can certainly choose to "fear no evil." You can choose to believe that God "is with me." You can let Him comfort you as He sets a table for you in the midst of your enemies of anxiety, apathy, sadness, loneliness, despair, or depression.

Replacing My Sadness with God's Joy

Joy is much deeper than happiness. Happiness depends on our circumstances. Joy shines in like a ray of light into the darkness of despair. Joy is the truth of who God is. *Joy is a settled confidence in the goodness of God.* Joy is living in God's presence—fully alive.

As you and I choose to live and walk in the presence of God, His joy will win over every dark thought. Joy is not the absence of pain. Jesus Himself felt pain on the cross, but Hebrews 12:2 says,

> *Joy is a settled confidence in the goodness of God.*

"We do this by keeping our eyes on Jesus,
the champion who initiates and perfects our faith.
Because of the joy *awaiting him, he endured*

the cross, disregarding its shame.
Now he is seated in the place of honor beside God's throne."
Hebrews 12:2, NLT

Jesus knew joy awaited Him. You are destined for that same joy. Deep, satisfying, fulfilling joy designed by God is the culmination of your journey. But you don't have to wait for it. It is also a fuel. Joy neutralizes restless discontent and energizes purposeful pursuit—and it's yours now.

Nothing steal God's joy. A rainy day does not squelch His delight in you or the world that He made. God does not become concerned with delays or setbacks. He is above time. He lives in eternity. God is not easily hurt. He never becomes offended. God's joy is an eternal peace that consequences or circumstance cannot quench.

The joy of the Lord is the strength of every Life-Giving Mom. Replace your sadness with His joy! Joy is the life-giving, hope-filling, peace-making presence of God. Our joy is ultimately found in our relationship with God. He is the only One who truly satisfies. He is the One who can make your soul content.

Radical joy is a choice of daily gratitude. Gone are your moments of entitled living. Here to stay is the ever-present reality of God With Us, Emmanuel. At Christmas when we sing "Joy to the World" we are celebrating the triumphant victory of God coming in the flesh. He came down to earth to be one of us. He knows our pain. He suffered and bled and died for us.

Move forward with faith-filled and power-packed celebration of God's joy. Expect His joy in unexpected places and faces. His joy is contagious. It swallows up sorrow and pain with the wonder of who He is.

So let joy move you like it once did. Get rid of your cynical attitudes, and truly experience His joy!

A PRAYER FOR
Joy

I COME TO YOU LORD IN WEAKNESS.

LIFE CAN WEIGH ME DOWN AT TIMES,

BUT YOU ARE MY JOY AND MY STRENGTH.

I CAN TURN TO YOU WHEN ALL ELSE FAILS.

I CAN COME TO YOU IN SADNESS, WEEPING, AND CRYING.

YOU WIPE AWAY MY TEARS WITH YOUR PROMISES.

HELP ME TO LOOK UP TO YOU, GOD.

YOU ARE MY SHIELD OF PROTECTION.

YOU ARE MY STRONG TOWER.

YOU ARE MY HOPE.

TODAY I CHOOSE TO SURRENDER MY LIFE TO YOU.

I PUT IN YOUR HANDS MY DAILY NECESSITIES AND NEEDS.

I BELIEVE YOU TO TURN MY SORROW INTO DANCING.

I TAKE OFF MY HEAVY COAT OF DREAD.

I TRUST YOU TO CLOTHE ME WITH GLADNESS.

WEEPING MAY LAST DURING THE NIGHT TIME,

BUT YOUR JOY COMES IN THE MORNING.

I PUT MY HOPE IN YOU, GOD.

YOU ARE MY JOY AND DELIGHT.

(PSALM 16, 30, 43)

 Download written prayers at **www.SueDetweiler.com**.

Peace

—❦—

Tranquil, calm, restful;
quietness of heart and soul.
Peace is serenity and solitude
laced in contentment.
Peace brings harmony in relationships.
Peace fills cleansed hearts,
from toxic thoughts and emotions.
Peace heals toxic wounds.
Peace is freedom from disturbance.
It is a mental calm and a quiet mind.
Peace brings a cessation of strife.
Peace is healthy prosperity,
good fortune, and a humble heart.
It is unburdened bliss with rest-filled happiness.
Walking daily with the Prince of Peace,
Jesus.

Chapter 4

REPLACING MY ANXIETY

WITH GOD'S PEACE

One morning when I was standing at the kitchen sink with my hands in dishwater, my husband, Wayne, said, "Sue, we got the announcement yesterday. American Eagle Airlines is closing its doors in Nashville. Everyone is being laid off."

Panic began to spread up the back of my neck. This had been a second job for Wayne to supplement our income as pastors. However, we had resigned the church that we had pastored for nine years and were in transition. This was the job that was helping to feed our four daughters, ages 6, 4, 2, and newborn.

I was silent for a moment as my mind raced. *What are we going to do? How are we going to live? I need to stay home with my daughters. I can't get a job now.*

I shook the dishwater off my hands and turned to Wayne, praying that God would give me words that would help. I sensed God giving me the words to say to encourage my faithful husband.

"Honey, it must mean that promotion is around the corner for you." There was a precious moment of peace reflected in my hardworking husband's eyes. He was thankful for my words. He knew I believed in him. He was working overtime to make ends meet.

Reeling from the news, I took off for my early morning prayer walk. I gave God my long list of concerns. As I prayed I started to become more anxious as the reality of our situation began to set in. I ended my conversation with, "And God, we need groceries!"

As I moved through my morning routine with my daughters, I was surprised at lunch time when an acquaintance showed up with four bags of groceries. She didn't know that my husband was losing his job, but God did. My new friend simply said, "I was praying this morning, and God just put you guys on my heart. I thought you might need this." Tears filled my eyes as I received her inspired act of kindness.

Amazed at God's specific answer to my prayer, peace began to fill my anxious heart. *God, if you can answer my simple, faith-filled request for groceries, You can do anything!*

As I put the groceries on the shelf of our humble pantry, God reminded me of my prayer to Him the week before. I had visited Wayne at the airport where he worked. This job had been great as a secondary income for our growing family. He especially appreciated having flying benefits so that we could visit our families.

The previous week, while watching Wayne work in the cold, dark room where he threw bags on a conveyer belt, I cried out to God. *My husband is made for more than this. He is a seminary graduate. You have made him to pastor people. Lord, get my husband out of here!*

Now, here we were a week later. Oops. I didn't mean for Wayne to lose his job. I was asking God to promote him. That's why the words "promotion must be around the corner" came out of my mouth. I was able to say those words because I had been praying them over my husband.

Parenting Through Anxious Times

Life is filled with surprising twists and turns. As a mom, it may feel like you are whitewater rafting with your whole family. There you are floating down the river, and all of a sudden you are headed for a waterfall. You make sure that the life preservers are buckled around every child, and you paddle hard. Ultimately, you are trusting God through everything.

Parenting is not done in a vacuum. There are always things you and/or your husband may be facing. If you are a single mom, you carry a double load of stress.

> *In Jesus' last words to His disciples He warned them that life would not be "smooth sailing."*

So how do you keep your anxious thoughts from becoming a toxic swamp in your mind, polluting everyone around you? I have a one word answer: *prayer*.

In Jesus' last words to His disciples He warned them that life would not be "smooth sailing." But He also promised them peace.

*"I have told you these things, so that in Me you
may have [perfect] peace and confidence. In the world
you have tribulation and trials and distress and frustration;
but be of good cheer [take courage; be confident,
certain, undaunted]! For I have overcome
the world. [I have deprived it of power to
harm you and have conquered it for you.]"*
John 16:33, AMP

He gave us His Word so that you and I can have perfect peace and confidence. In the same breath He promised that we would have tribulation, trials, distress, and frustration. Then He instructs us to take courage, be confident, certain, undaunted!

How can He expect you to be undaunted in the midst of distress? He simply says, "I have overcome the world!" He is the overcomer. He will help you overcome every trial. At the cross, He deprived the enemy of power over you. Whatever situation you are presently facing, it has no power to harm you. He conquered it for you.

> He is the Prince of Peace, so if you walk with Him, you will experience His peace.

This just makes me want to shout! His promise of peace in our lives is not a rinky-dink promise of superficial pats on the back. He walks with us through trying situations. He is the Prince of Peace, so if you walk with Him, you will experience His peace.

The Promise of Peace

I wish I could give you a passcode to avoid every toxic situation you are going to experience in your life as a mom. I also don't want you to think I am writing this book to sound like I am now free from all trials, and I have arrived at the safe harbor of peace!

No, just taking a step out of the boat into the water to write this book has seemed to bring about a storm of resistance. Just over the weekend while I was writing this manuscript, my 17-year-old son flipped the car that he was driving his 13-year-old brother in. Less than 24 hours later, my 23-year-old daughter and her fiancée were almost crushed by a semi-truck. I give credit to God and the power of prayer that all of them are safe.

Yet, I know some of you who are reading this chapter have lost children to miscarriage, abortion, car accidents, disease, abuse, and situations beyond your control. You may be dealing with the same sense of helplessness I felt when I was unable to save my own daughter from a house fire. You may be in the middle of a broken relationship that is causing you great emotional pain.

I wish I held the key to give you a stress-free existence. In this world, we all face trial. The good news is we don't go through it alone. Jesus is the One who is in the boat with us. He is the One calming the storm. So cry out to Him in prayer!

To replace your anxiety with His unshakeable peace requires you to trust Him. Choose to take heart and put your focus on the fact that Jesus overcame, so you can, too. He is the God of peace who crushes anxiety under your feet!

> *"The God of peace will soon crush Satan under your feet.*
> *May the grace of our Lord Jesus be with you."*
> Romans 16:20, NLT

God gives His grace to you in times of your greatest need. His unmerited favor surprises me every time. It never fails to amaze me how God chooses to answer my prayers.

Answered Prayer

With my husband's loss of his airport job, he was able to serve in a greater capacity at the growing church that we became a part of. We became small group leaders, and in our second meeting we had 64 people in attendance (25 were children). We were surprised by God's favor.

A few months later my husband was in a balcony of a church that was being dedicated, and our senior pastor was on the platform.

Our senior pastor looked up and saw my faithful husband and sensed God saying, "This is a man that has been tried by fire. He is pure gold. Bring him on your pastoral team. He will help many people."

God opened the door for Wayne to serve on a growing church staff with a generous and visionary senior pastor. A short time later I also joined the team and was able to use my gifts and still keep my priorities of being a mom. God is amazing! We experienced many fruitful years of ministry together. God provided.

Don't Give Up!

Anxiety is a deceiver. Like a blowfish that expands to make itself look bigger than it really is, anxiety exaggerates every bad thing that could happen. Worry will convince you that you can't make it. What happens to a mom when she gives up? What happens to her children?

> Worry will convince you that you can't make it.

One day as I pushed my stroller in my neighborhood I met another mom. I visited with her and her children in their home for about an hour. Since my husband and I were pastors, our neighborhood felt like a "parish" to me, so I regularly made "house calls" on neighbors. Our neighborhood was a suburb of new homes with white picket fences and hopes for the future.

My neighbor appeared stressed, but nothing out of the ordinary compared to the other moms I visited with. Her daughters were beautiful with golden hair. They loved play jewelry, ribbons, and Barbies. After that initial meeting I kept in touch with the mom, but only by waving my hand or sharing brief words on the street as I walked by pushing my baby stroller.

One morning I awoke to the tragic news that she had taken her life and the life of her children. She had driven her car with her children in it to a nearby lake, and everyone drowned. I share her story here, not remembering her name or even the exact number of her children, or the details of her death from twenty years ago. I feel regret that I had not done more to help her.

How does a mom, called as a life-giver, become a life-destroyer? I felt so helpless in this situation and somehow responsible. It doesn't take much of an Internet search to find headlines of other mothers taking the life of a child or multiple children:

"Mom Drowns Children"
"Children Die in House Fire while Mom is at Work"
"Mom Kills Kids for Talking Back"

If you are reading *9 Traits of a Life-Giving Mom,* you not only desire to be a Life-Giving Mom, but you probably feel like you need help to replace your worst with God's best. If we are honest, we all need help. Life can get really hard, and if we don't have a strategy of wholeness for our children and ourselves, we will pass on death rather than life.

Life-Giving Moms
Walk in God's Peace

To walk in God's peace, a Life-Giving Mom must regularly detoxify her mind and emotions. Here is a list of detoxifying habits that have helped restore God's peace in my life:

- **Reading the Bible** (Replacing the world's words with God's Word.)
- **Prayer & Meditation** (Replacing my concerns with God's care.)
- **Forgiveness** (Replacing my hurt with God's health.)
- **Journaling** (Reframing tough situations with God's strategy.)

- **Church Community** (Replacing my apathy with God's passion.)
- **Books** (Replacing my confusion with God's clarity.)
- **Podcasts** (Restoring my foggy brain with God's focus.)
- **Conferences** (Reshaping my weakness with God's power.)
- **Counseling** (Rebuilding my brokenness with God's wholeness.)

> *God's peace establishes order and balance in your life and home.*

You may need the help of a pastor, coach, or counselor to help you detoxify from traumatic events in your life. For me, receiving prayer counseling after the fire set me on a path of peace to be a Life-Giving Mom. It was like someone had lifted up a shade and let light into my life. Every area of my life improved. I was a completely new person.

God's peace establishes order and balance in your life and home. God's peace is a tangible force that overwhelms overwrought emotions with God's powerful presence. His peace anchors your thoughts and steadies your emotions. His peace strengthens your ability as a Life-Giving Mom to face stress-filled situations with calm serenity.

Replacing your anxiety with God's peace is a moment-by-moment choice to view God as bigger than your problem. God's peace is the absence of inner conflict and turmoil. God's peace is embracing the character of Jesus, who is the Prince of Peace.

WATCH
Watch the free video
Replacing My Anxiety with God's Peace
at www.SueDetweiler.com.

A PRAYER FOR
Peace

———⊶⊷———

PRINCE OF PEACE,
SHEPHERD OF MY HEART AND SOUL.
LEAD ME IN YOUR WAYS.
GUIDE ME ON YOUR PATHS.
HELP ME TO TURN AWAY FROM THE SWAMP
OF ANXIETY, WORRY, AND DREAD.
SHOW ME HOW TO LIVE PEACE-FILLED, TRANQUIL DAYS.
THANK YOU FOR HEALTHY THOUGHTS AND REFLECTIONS.
I WILL MEDITATE ON WHAT IS NOBLE AND RIGHT.
I KNOW THAT AS I PRAY ABOUT EVERYTHING,
YOUR PEACE WILL GUARD MY HEART AND MIND.
YOUR PEACE EXCEEDS ANYTHING I COULD UNDERSTAND,
SO I WILL FIX MY MIND ON WHAT IS LOVELY.
I WILL CELEBRATE WHAT IS ADMIRABLE.
DAILY, I REJOICE IN YOUR PEACE.
(PHILIPPIANS 4:4-8)

———⊶⊷———

Download written prayers at **www.SueDetweiler.com.**

Patience

—⸝⸝⸝—

It is calm self-restraint.
Patience is composure, understanding,
perseverance, and endurance.
It is tenacity of mind and heart.
Patience is the staying power and resolve of love.
Patience is the capacity to accept and tolerate delay or trouble.
It quietly endures difficult circumstances.
It perseveres without acting annoyed.
Patience is steadfast.
Patience is immovable.
Patience is being able to wait a while longer.
It bears with another's weakness.
It humbly relies on God
for His Word, His Will,
and His TIME.
Patience is the mark
of a man who is filled with the fruit
of the Holy Spirit.

Chapter 5

REPLACING MY FRUSTRATION
WITH GOD'S PATIENCE

My thoughts began to swirl around me as I paced the floor with a baby on my hip. *I feel trapped…I have to get out of here…Where is he?…He is always late…*

The accusations began to build momentum with the ticking of the clock. By the time my husband walked in the door, I jammed the baby in his arms and ran out. Oh, the joy of a walk! All by myself! No one pulling on me…crying…needing something.

He has no idea how this feels…I am going crazy…When do I have any time for me…

Being a mom can vacillate between the sweetness of hugs and kisses to feeling like you are in jail. Taking care of children at home may have meant that you gave up your job and income. As moms we have less time, less money, and often less encouragement. If you are like me, your face hasn't had make-up on it in days. In the early days of motherhood you are lucky if you get a shower. You have to lock the door to go to the bathroom alone.

Feeling trapped often prompts us to blame someone else for our plight. You may blame your kids. You may blame your husband, who gets to go to work every day. Or if your husband stays home, you may still blame him because you have to work. You think back to when you had prayed for a child. You asked God for this. *Ugh! If you had only known about the constant frustrations.*

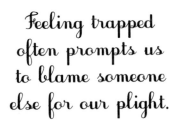

Feeling trapped often prompts us to blame someone else for our plight.

Of course, there are the other times when the sweetness of being together fills your love tank until it overflows with good thoughts and good memories. Your child falls asleep in your arms. The purity of the moment floods you with joy.

Are moms schizophrenic? How can you feel like the most blessed woman in the world one day, and the next moment you are a ranting lunatic?

What is going on? Is this motherhood? I thought it would be so much more. Why didn't anyone tell me it would be this hard?

One day when I was particularly frustrated with a petty issue, I happened to read 1 Peter 5 in *The Amplified Bible* which says,

> *"…Clothe (apron) yourselves, all of you, with humility
> [as the garb of a servant, so that its covering cannot possibly
> be stripped from you, with freedom from pride and arrogance]
> toward one another. For God sets Himself against the proud
> (the insolent, the overbearing, the disdainful, the presumptuous,
> the boastful)—[and He opposes, frustrates, and defeats
> them], but gives grace (favor, blessing) to the humble.
> Therefore humble yourselves [demote, lower yourselves*

in your own estimation] under the mighty hand of God,
that in due time He may exalt you."
1 Peter 5:5b-6, AMP

Well, I could relate to being clothed like a servant. My daily garb was sweatpants, and my adornment was a ponytail. Like a servant, I dealt with dirt, dishes, and diapers. What it said next got my attention. God opposes and *frustrates* the proud. That's when it hit me. My lack of patience with my children had to do with my *frustration* that resulted from pride. It was God Himself who put His foot in the door of my pride.

As my mind, heart, and spirit meditated on this Scripture, I realized my husband and children were not causing my frustration. I was choosing to be frustrated. Each arrogant thought fueled my irritation.

On the days that I set out to serve God, my husband, and my children we would all experience God's peace. When I humbled myself and lowered myself, I received the grace, favor, and blessing of the humble. The fruit of my humble walk with God was patience.

A picture of bowing before God as a servant came to me as I performed the menial jobs of a mom. I saw God's smile as He opened for me the door of His grace to walk through. No longer did I feel impatient because I couldn't accomplish everything I wanted to in a day. The fruit of patience made me laugh at the silly antics of my children. I could laugh at their spaghetti faces as I wiped their spaghetti fingerprints from the walls.

I began to hear sweet phrases in my ear, spoken during my times of early morning prayer. One morning when I was pouring my heart out to God at not being able to accomplish all that I wanted to, I heard this phrase: "There is enough time in the day to do everything I have called you to."

Wow, maybe my checklist isn't God's checklist?!

I began to relax. I didn't have to get it all done. I just needed to be in God's presence as I cared for my children. I began to have more fun and enjoy life as my character became more like Christ's.

A Call to Character

Character is developed through an intimate walk with God. As moms we need to learn to walk with God in a new way. Before you had children you could get up and work-out, or take a walk whenever you wanted to. You could reflect and get your mind together before anyone demanded something from you. You had time to pray and read your Bible. You had the freedom to spend time with your husband or friends.

> *Character is developed through an intimate walk with God.*

As a mom you no longer have the same freedom. You are on call 24/7. What is the new normal for you? What is the new way for you to live a balanced life? Is it possible to have balance *and* have children?

As I had more children, I began to build strategies into my daily routine so that I would not end up pushed to the edge. If I could build times of health and godly meditation and reflection into my life, I could do more than survive. I could thrive.

Reading the Bible became my lifeline. Gone were the moments of having uninterrupted time whenever I wanted to spend time with God. Now I had to strategize, fight for this time, and improvise.

I kept my Bible handy with a bookmark in it, ready to read when I nursed the baby. I would even put the Bible on the floor in my bathroom and flip my head over to blow dry my hair and read the

Word. I began to take prayer walks with the double-wide stroller. I would pray out loud with a prayer list in my hands.

I began to turn the worship music up high in the house and take dance breaks with kids in my arms. This was my dance of survival on days that were rough.

Building daily structures into our lives and homes become pleasant boundaries of health. Taking the children to the YMCA with me so that I could get exercise was important for my mental health.

The most important boundary for me was setting aside a time that I was alone with God. One morning Angela woke up and was pulling on my arm.

"Mommy, I want breakfast," she said.

"Mommy has to eat first. Then I will get you breakfast," I answered.

Angela looked puzzled and began to look around for the hidden food that I might be eating. All she could see was my Bible on my lap.

"Do you eat the Bible for breakfast, Momma?"

I laughed and kissed her.

> *I began to find that when I didn't make time for God at the beginning of the day, I struggled.*

"That's right, sweetie. Mommy has to eat the Bible first. Then I can make you breakfast." That gave me ten more minutes.

I began to find that when I didn't make time for God at the beginning of the day, I struggled. With daughters ages 6, 4, 2, and newborn, I would be hanging by my fingernails until my husband got home each night. With a lack of sleep, I was at my worst and easily irritated. I could become uptight by anything that inconvenienced me.

If you have patience with your children, you won't jerk them around while buckling their car seat. If you have patience, you won't scream at them in irritation or glare at them in anger. If you have patience, you won't shake or slap your child. If you walk in patience as a Life-Giving Mom, you will discipline your children in the balance of grace, wisdom, insight, and truth.

Every Life-Giving Mom is Unique

You do not need to feel like you are pressed in a mold to look picture perfect as a Life-Giving Mom. You may have one child, or you may have many. You may work, or you may stay home with your children. You may be single, or you may be married. Your children may have been sheltered, or they may have been wounded and abused. No one but God knows your unique challenges and pain that develops the character of long-suffering into your life.

This I know: if you are a mom, you have experienced pain. For most of us, we have experienced ripping, life-altering pain. You don't really know bittersweet pain until you are a mom. You hurt when your child is rejected. You hurt when you make mom-mistakes. You hurt when you face adult challenges that your child would never understand.

If you are not healed, then your own hurt will hurt your child. Patience is the process God has for all of us to take the issues of pain and suffering and turn them into the sweetness of sacrifice and servanthood.

A Life-Giving Mom is patient and long-suffering. Patience is the ability to endure delay, difficulty, or discomfort. It is to be tolerant of annoyance with calm resolve. To be a patient mom is to understand

If you are not healed, then your own hurt will hurt your child.

the unique stresses of a child and to be persevering, constant, and consistent. Patience is not being rash, hasty, or impulsive. It is not easily provoked. A mom is able to suffer long with her child.

Learning Patience Through Pain

The patience of a Life-Giving Mom begins during pregnancy and birth. A mom suffers through her body expanding and being overtaken by the life inside of her. Every hormone is off-kilter. Her hunger and need for sleep increases. Nesting instincts encourage every mom to think about the needs of her coming child. During labor, her body is being ripped as she pushes life out of her womb into the world.

The bliss of giving birth to a baby is covered with the blood of childbirth. Pain precedes life. A patient mom endures the pain because of the life she will hold in her arms.

One of the first things that a mother hears when the baby is born is the cry of her child. As the bonding takes place between mother and child, it is the cry of her newborn that signals the milk glands of her breasts to secrete milk. It's the very cry of our children that motivates a mom to feed and care for her child.

A Life-Giving Mom is Also Patient with Herself

Sometimes it is the simplest of things that restore peace and order to a mom's perspective. A warm shower and a good meal. A loving adult conversation. A pedicure or a shopping trip. A night out with someone you love. The wonder of enjoying positive, upbuilding, gratifying life experiences will lift anyone's mood.

Patience provides an opportunity to slow down and enjoy your everyday life. Patience laughs at your mom-moments. Patience allows you and your child to grow in the pace of grace. Patience is enjoying your child and not letting the "work" of life get in your way of fun. Patience is valuing each child as precious in God's sight and priceless to you. Patience recognizes the time needed for a deeply wounded child to find safety in the arms of a parent. Patience trusts God with the result of the time spent and the seeds sown.

> *Patience is valuing each child as precious in God's sight and priceless to you.*

WATCH
Watch the free video
Replacing My Frustration with God's Patience
at www.SueDetweiler.com.

A PRAYER FOR
Patience

———⊶⊷———

Loving Heavenly Father,
You alone are perfect.
I give you my own imperfections.
I ask you to forgive me of my Pride.
Open up your door of grace and favor
as I bow my heart to serve you.
I humble myself and
get dressed as a servant.
I choose to serve You
as I serve my children.
Clothe me with humility, wit, and humor.
Fill me with the Fruit of Patience
as I choose to walk in your
Presence as a mom and steward
of this precious life that You have
entrusted to my hands.
I love You, God. I trust You!

———⊶⊷———

Kindness

———✦———

Kindness is friendly warmth.
Kindness is always generous and considerate.
It gives in service.
Kindness is affectionate concern.
It is helpful thoughtfulness.
Kindness is unselfish.
It is compassionate and holds sympathy and
charitable understanding close.
Kindness is big-heartedness.
Kindness has concern for others.
Kindness does random loving acts.
It's always helping others.
Kindness cultivates caring.
It is devoted loyalty, and the
tender mercies of God.
Kindness is love in motion.

Chapter 6

REPLACING MY NEGATIVITY
WITH GOD'S KINDNESS

"I love you," Alexandre (Dre) said in English. Everyone's eyes flooded with tears, from the Brazilian judge and the psychologist to the social worker and the translator.

"*Eu te amo*," I said in Portuguese as tears dripped down my face. Dre had captured the room with the universal language of love. I plopped Ezequiel (Zeke) on my lap as he looked up with a shy grin.

Abandoned and orphaned early in life, we adopted Dre and Zeke when they were already 12 and 8 years old. Sitting in the darkened courthouse room in a tiny village of Brazil we learned more details of the trauma our sons had already experienced. Our sons were born to us out of that womb of understanding. They walked into our lives with old clothes, broken sandals, and all they owned in a Spider-Man backpack.

As mothers, we have the unique privilege of partnering with God to give life to our children. Our sons did not have the safety and refuge of being born into a life-giving family. Sharing love with our sons was not as simple as bonding with our daughters at birth. They were not held, cuddled, and looked at as babies.

If you met Dre and Zeke now, it would be difficult for our sons to look you in the eye. They still arch their backs when hugged and pull away from touch.

How different Dre's arrival into our home than the arrival of his sister, Sarah. Both of them were born the same year, only six months apart.

Looking back at Sarah's arrival into our home, I remember the sun streaming in through the windows and dancing on the cheeks of our four daughters. Weakened by the delivery of Sarah Faith, I sat propped up in bed as Rachel (age 6) and Angela (age 4) nestled close. It was 2-year-old Hannah who pushed everyone out of the way to get her turn at holding "my baby."

What a stunning contrast found in the utter delight of welcoming the miracle of a newborn into the circle of safety and familial love. All of us were looking intently at Sarah. We welcomed her. We loved her. We cherished her. But it didn't happen that way for our sons when they were born.

Rather than being celebrated and cared for, Dre and Zeke were left to fend for themselves in Brazil. At an early age most orphans have suffered abandonment, loss, rejection, poverty, and sometimes indifference. The basic needs every child has to be held, fed, cared for, and loved have been denied an orphan at some level. The wounding of many orphans begins while they are in the womb of their biological mothers, who may be taking drugs and drinking alcohol. God's Word says,

> *"Pure and genuine religion in the sight of God the Father means **caring for orphans** and widows **in their distress** and refusing to let the world corrupt you."*
> James 1:27, NLT

Caring for orphans in their distress by adopting them into your home opens the door to another level of pain that most North Americans are either unwilling or unable to endure. I understand. *Believe me, I do not judge people for their desire to adopt only children ages 3 and under. Nor do I judge people who choose never to adopt. I understand the costs involved.*

All I can say is that my heart for the abandoned older children in the world was broken and filled with God's heart, which He expresses in Psalm 68:

> *"**Father to the fatherless**, defender of widows*
> *—this is God, whose dwelling is holy.*
> ***God places the lonely in families; he sets the***
> ***prisoners free and gives them joy.***
> *But he makes the **rebellious live in a sun-scorched land**."*
> Psalm 68:5-6, NLT

God opened my eyes to the needs of older orphans in 2008 when Wayne and I went away to a lake house to pray and seek God on whether we were called to adopt. I found myself weeping a lot as we began to research adoption of children in Brazil.

"God places the lonely in families..."

There is an overwhelming need for older children to be adopted, especially in Brazil. We read articles on the internet about off-duty police officers being hired by the wealthy merchants in Brazil to shoot the orphans living on the streets. This was not a one-time event but a cycle that provides extra income for the underpaid police force.

God was breaking my heart for orphans in Brazil. He was also opening my heart to adopt older children. Most adoptions are of children under the age of three. Most people do not want to deal with the severity of the wounds of older children. God was softening my heart with my tears.

At the end of the week, our teenage daughters came to the lake house with my mom. They knew we had gone away to pray. Our oldest daughter, Rachel, said, "We knew it was a big deal. We didn't know if we would move to India as missionaries or if we would plant a church. We just knew Dad and Mom were asking God about a 'big question.'"

We began to share with our children our reflections about adoption. We did not come to the table with our older children with a predetermined decision. We felt like they would be a part of the journey, and they needed to be a part of the decision-making.

As we went around the table talking with our daughters, our youngest, Sarah Faith, made us all laugh through our tears. In a matter-of-fact tone she said, "I'm for it. Even with all the work of adoption." We just laughed, having no idea how much work it would be.

You may not be called to adopt, but you will be called to show God's kindness to your children. Part of being a Life-Giving Mom is rolling up your sleeves and wading into the messy parts of life. Being a Life-Giving Mom does not guarantee having children who make life-giving choices. There are no perfect children, and you won't be a perfect

> *Being a Life-Giving Mom does not guarantee having children who make life-giving choices.*

mom. You will wrestle with your own mistakes and weep at the poor choices of those you love most.

God's Kindness

The fruit of kindness is a remarkable force of persuasion in the lives of our children. Kindness is the quality of being friendly, generous, and considerate. To be warmhearted, affectionate, and caring with our children teaches them about the nature of God.

God's kindness is extended to each one of us. All of us would be orphans if God had not adopted us.

All of us would be orphans if God had not adopted us.

> *"So you have not received a spirit that makes*
> *you fearful slaves. Instead, you received God's Spirit*
> *when he adopted you as his own children.*
> *Now we call him, "Abba, Father."*
> *For his Spirit joins with our spirit to affirm*
> *that we are God's children.*
> *And since we are his children, we are his heirs.*
> *In fact, together with Christ we are heirs of God's glory.*
> *But if we are to share his glory, we must also share his suffering."*
> Romans 8:15-17, NLT

God's kindness is seen in that He does not treat us like fearful slaves. We respond to His kindness by calling Him "Abba," "Father," or "Daddy." In a similar way, when we come to God as our Father, we are receiving our inheritance as His children.

God's kindness is not based on my behavior. The only prerequisite for being adopted by God is that we receive Jesus. His kindness and goodness lead us to repentance (See Romans 2:4). Romans 5:6 says, "When we were utterly helpless, Christ came at just the right time and died for us sinners" (NLT). We do not earn His kindness, He simply gives it to us because He is good.

Overcoming My Negativity

As a mom, I replace my negativity with God's kindness every time I instruct my child without condemnation or judgment. I replace negativity when I choose to be loving and keep no record of wrong (See 1 Corinthians 13). I replace my negativity with His kindness when I seek to understand where the heart of my child is rather than think the worst about him or her.

God has given parents the unique opportunity to represent God to our children. We are not only charged to instruct them in God's ways, but to share His heart.

As a mom I have been too *results-oriented* and not enough *process-oriented*. I wanted the result of well-behaved children with great manners and a spotless house where everyone did their chores. These are good goals. However, the most important is that my children feel loved and learn how to reverence God and His ways.

I was able to turn a corner when I thought about the needs of my sons. I realized that their hearts were like an overdrawn bank account. In the morning they did not start with zero in their love-bank. They started with negative ten. I noticed that if I was positive throughout the day, they would end the day with about plus five. However, when they woke up the next day, they did not start with plus five in their love-bank. They were back to negative ten. It was

Only God can fill the leak in my child's love tank.

like their love-bank had a continual hole in it that caused them to
have a negative balance.

Only God can fill the leak in my child's love-tank. God's kindness
never ends. Even when God is instructing us as His children, He is
not harsh or rude. He does not have a look of disappointment on
His face when he looks at me. He is not shaking his head saying in
an exasperated voice, "What am I going to do with her? She did it
again!"

Jesus represented the Father to us best. When He came to earth
He did not celebrate the fact that the Pharisees followed God's law.
He was concerned about their hearts. You do not see Jesus using
negative words or actions to put down those who were caught in sin.
He was constantly helping them up.

It was the religious crowd that Jesus challenged. He spoke
against the Pharisees, the Sadducees, and the Scribes. He gave words
of grace, healing, and forgiveness to the woman caught in adultery
and the woman with the alabaster flask.

Showing God's Kindness

Showing God's kindness to children is valuing them and treating
them with respect. To be kind to is to develop a compassionate
empathy to show them you truly care. Kindness is being considerate,
thoughtful, unselfish, and friendly.

A Life-Giving Mom hears the cry of her child no matter where
they are on the earth. The Thanksgiving and Christmas before
adopting, I began to long for my sons. It was like I could hear the cry
of their hearts. Adoption was only a nine-month process for us since
we were adopting two brothers who had been in an orphanage most
of their lives. The only significant bond Dre and Zeke had was with
each other. We found out when we arrived in Brazil that they would
have split the brothers up if we had not arrived in their lives.

Their first Christmas in the United States was amazing. They were excited about everything. They had never seen snow before and danced in the driveway with the Tennessee snowflakes landing in their hair. They loved decorating the tree and were amazed at the ornaments.

When Dre and Zeke began to open their gifts, the smiles on their faces lit up the room. It was then that Zeke shared in his Portuguese/English that the Christmas before he had prayed for a family. In the orphanage they didn't have a Christmas dinner, nor did they open any Christmas presents. It was just a day that they didn't go to school. I remembered then the longing in my heart the Christmas before for these sons whom God would place in our home. How awesome of God to answer the prayer of an orphan for a family.

Falling into
Negative Parenting Traps

As you and I journey together to replace our worst with God's best, we need to acknowledge the times that we fall into negative parenting traps. A book called *Negative Parenting Tips: How to Wound Your Child Through Neglect, Emotional Instability, Harsh Correction, and Over-Permissiveness* would not be a bestseller. Unless we make intentional choices of how we will parent our children, we will often follow in our own parents' footsteps. We have read their manual of parenting through example.

> We need to acknowledge the times that we fall into negative parenting traps.

Upon adopting our sons, we were not beginning at ground zero with them. Every day we started at negative ten. In addition to their need for safety and bonding, we found it tough that there were negative habits in their lives that we were constantly instructing them on. It was obvious our instruction was being received as negative criticism when Zeke said, "You're mean."

At a particularly stressful time when we were getting our home ready to sell, Zeke and Dre were not cooperating. We had a large amount of work to do. One of our family values in the Detweiler house is that we all pitch in and work hard to get a project done. Hard work is a part that Dre and Zeke had not embraced fully.

I came around the corner and found Zeke goofing off. With a very harsh tone and an angry look on my face I got really close to Zeke, and I pointed my finger at him and said, "Enough!"

At almost the same instance I heard deep in my spirit the voice of God speaking to me saying, "Enough!" It was a strong impression, so I later pulled away with my Bible and journal to reflect on my own actions and attitudes toward Zeke.

There are times that I will journal my prayers to God and then take time to listen and write down any wisdom from heaven that I sense. As I was journaling, I saw that my own attitude of critical approach to the situation was damaging Zeke and creating distance in our relationship. Lots of boys don't like to work. My attitude and actions were just shaming him and not motivating him in a positive direction.

God's kindness to all of us is shown in His grace toward us.

God's kindness to all of us is shown in His grace toward us. He is kind when we don't deserve it. Even when He is firm with us, He is never unkind. His heart and His words always display the unmerited favor of His grace. He always values our personhood even when He is instructing us in His Word.

You and I must consistently show the kindness of God to our kids. We can't do this in our own strength. We need God's divine enabling to walk with tender care toward each child. I wish I could say this was the only time I needed to apologize to my son. It was not. I regularly need to ask God to help me and show me how to parent His children His way.

Turning Away from the Negative Cycle

Each child is unique. In order for each child to receive God's kindness through us, it needs to be packaged in a way that they can receive it. So I tried an experiment. Rather than beginning the day with correcting Dre or Zeke for the chores that were left undone, I made a point to speak five positive things in a row to each of my sons early in the morning and throughout the day.

The positive affirmation showed on the face of my oldest. His smile is a rare treat. When Dre smiles, the whole room is lit by the power of it. As I concentrated on the positive, they were less defensive and resistant when I needed to instruct them.

How much are you affirming your kids' value? It's probably easy to affirm and rejoice in your children when they are making positive choices. It is easy to let the light in your eyes delight over them when there is a positive connection between you, but what about when your relationship is strained?

Think about your time with your children. Do you spend more time trying to instruct them about their behavior and miss opportunities for positive affirmation? Do you have time to play and do fun things with them? Do you take time to learn what they like and enjoy? Do you make consistent and special efforts to show God's kindness to your kids?

The negative parenting trap is when your negative thoughts about your child and their behavior begin to be exaggerated in your mind. The problem they are facing becomes urgent in your mind. You may begin to parent them out of fear. Rather than a smile on your own face, the lines in your forehead and your frown lines become pronounced.

Do you make consistent and special efforts to show God's kindness?

Your children will sense your own emotional instability and negativity. Even babies and toddlers can sense unpredictability in your care and feel less safe. Your children may not react instantly to your harsh criticism, but if it is a constant pressure, it will have a negative impact on your relationship. If you're overly permissive in your home and set no boundaries it will also negatively impact your home.

Think through the negative cycles you personally may have with your children. If you have multiple children you could be on a positive path with one, but in a damaging pattern with another. There is hope. You can't control the choices of your children, but you can control how you relate to them. You can replace your negativity with God's kindness.

A couple of weeks ago my husband looked at me and said, "I had no idea how difficult it would be to adopt our sons."

I looked at him with a depth of knowledge in my heart and said, "I know what you mean, honey." I paused and reflected, "I am a better person and a better parent because of it."

God has used the hardship, pain, and sacrifice of the process of helping orphans become sons to mold our character to be more like Christ. The fruit of kindness in our lives is not only what we do, it is who we are becoming.

Abundant Life

When Wayne and I were praying about whether Dre and Zeke were to be our sons, my husband and I got down on our knees in our room. We had to give the adoption agency a final answer. We had not planned on adopting boys who were older, nor had we planned on adopting children with special needs. But when we knelt in prayer, we had a peaceful sense of God's confirming call.

"The thief does not come except to steal, and to kill, and to destroy."

When we said "Amen" I turned and looked at the time on our digital clock, which said 10:10. Immediately, I remembered what Jesus said in John 10:10:

> *"The thief does not come except to steal, and to kill, and to destroy. I have come that they may have life, and that they may have it more abundantly."*
> John 10:10, NKJV

This Scripture became a confirmation to me about our call to parent our sons. I still stand on this promise of abundant life for Dre and Zeke. Five years into their adoption, and it is still extremely tough.

I pray for abundant life for you in your own family. Remember, the American dream of having a large home, small family, and lots of extra cash is not necessarily God's dream of abundance. His ways are higher than our ways. His thoughts are higher than our thoughts (See Isaiah 55:8-9).

If the enemy has attacked your relationship with your children through his negative lies, I believe with you for truth to prevail. I pray that Jesus will redeem every difficult place with His promise of abundant life. I believe with you for family relationships that are life-giving.

Abundant life is answering God's call fully and completely. He gives us choices all along the path that He leads us. Adoption is one of the ways that God's kindness is shown to the lost, the broken, and the abandoned.

God's kindness will lead you into adventures of faith. The good news is that He equips those He calls. There is more than enough grace to receive God's promises. Embrace God's path for your family.

WATCH
Watch the free video
Replacing My Negativity with God's Kindness
at **www.SueDetweiler.com.**

A PRAYER FOR
Kindness

Father God,
Your kindness leads me to repentance.
You mercy calls me to places deep.
Your favor is everlasting.
You are Good.
I trust you on the Great Adventure
You are leading me on.
I will follow you even if Your path has surprises.
You are the Redeemer.
Your kindness is forever.
As You restore what was lost,
You grant me with your inheritance.
Just because I am Yours forever,
Your kindness will lead me into Your arms.
I will nestle close to Your heart
safe, protected, and at home
in your Presence forever and ever.
Amen.

 Download written prayers at www.SueDetweiler.com.

Goodness

⸺⤫⸺

Goodness is moral integrity.

Honesty and nobility is nothing without goodness.

Goodness is gracious tenderness and warmth of heart.

Goodness is a friend to the friendless,

It brings hope to the hopeless.

It speaks of mercy to the merciless.

The Fullness of the character of God is Goodness.

Goodness is virtue of excellence.

It is rightness of relationship.

Goodness stays above reproach.

Goodness is honorable. Goodness is noble.

It is extravagant generosity.

Goodness dwells deep in wisdom.

It is unfailing love.

Goodness stays steady and consistent.

It is the quality of God's nature and holiness.

God's daily benefits are goodness.

Goodness is never manipulating, intimidating, or controlling.

Goodness is never unkind or unthoughtful.

Goodness always wins over evil.

Goodness is never defeated.

It always stays constant, immovable, and true.

Chapter 7

REPLACING MY MANIPULATION
WITH GOD'S GOODNESS

I sat on my back porch weeping. After experiencing God's amazing and unmerited favor in Brazil, we returned to our 18-year-old daughter making choices that broke our hearts. We were caught off guard, not expecting what unfolded before us. As we sought counsel, we were advised to take a tough love approach and to give our daughter a choice to repent or to move out of our home. She chose to move out of our home. I was devastated.

Sitting on my porch weeping as I read the book of Job, I contemplated what I could have done differently. Although I had never said this out loud, I realized that I had falsely believed that if I were a diligent parent I would never experience my children making choices that would be so painful.

I had thought the Scripture, "Train up a child in the way he should go, and when is old he will not depart from it" was an ironclad promise rather than a proverbial truth.

Why do we suffer?

Why is there so much pain in parenting?
What could I have done differently?
What should we do now?
I feel all alone.

I picked up the phone and called a mature woman of God who had experienced the pain of the choices of an 18-year-old daughter. The fact that she knew my pain comforted me. As she talked about how God had restored their relationship, her words gave me fresh hope.

Hope in the Goodness of God

I don't know what heartbreaking situation you may be facing within your family as you read this book. Your child may be diagnosed with autism. You may be dealing with a rebellious child. You may

> When people walk into your home they should sense peace and harmony.

have a child fighting cancer. You may be in a difficult time in your marriage or going through a bitter divorce. You may be a single mom fighting to have enough time with your child. There is nothing more agonizing than trauma within the walls of your home.

Your home is designed by God to provide safety from the elements, to be a place that's warm and nourishing to every member of your family. When people walk into your home they should sense peace and harmony. The relationships within your home should be your closest and most intimate.

What happens to your emotional health...
- *when the warfare is within the walls of your home?*
- *when someone in the family is sick?*

- *when someone loses their job?*
- *when relationships are divided or broken?*
- *when you feel out of control?*

It's at these points—when you are at your lowest—that the enemy often attacks you from another direction. Within the walls of the Christian community where you should find refuge, help, and healing, you may be met with judgment, criticism, or indifference. I sincerely hope this is not the case for you. If it is, I am deeply sorry for your pain.

If you are feeling out of control, you may fall into the trap of being a control freak. Your mind may be tormented with "*what if...*" or "*if only...*" You may be drawn into negative conversations where you defend yourself because you feel backed against a wall.

God's Goodness Leads to Repentance

I look back at our "tough love" approach, and we would do things differently, knowing now that it is "*the goodness of God*" that leads to repentance (See Romans 2:4). We tried to force our way on our 18-year-old rather than realize that God Himself gave her the power of choice.

We were blinded to our own issues of pride, manipulation, and control. Our daughter's sin was magnified and exaggerated in our eyes. It makes me think of Jesus' parable where He warns us:

> *"And why worry about a speck in your friend's eye when you have*
> *a log in your own? How can you think of saying to your friend,*
> *'Let me help you get rid of that speck in your eye,' when*
> *you can't see past the log in your own eye?*
> *Hypocrite! First get rid of the log in your own eye; then you will*
> *see well enough to deal with the speck in your friend's eye."*
> Matthew 7:3-5, NLT

We were walking around with planks in our eyes, trying to get our daughter's speck. We couldn't see how our harsh, negative correction was like a plank hitting her in the head and hurting our relationship.

Jesus showed the goodness of God to those who had fallen. He did not condone the sin of the woman caught in adultery, neither did He cast stones at her. He found a different way.

Harsh words, strict discipline, and a controlling home life can backfire on well-meaning religious parents. We sounded holy and righteous. We were just "waiting for her to repent."

Yesterday, my daughter and I sat together reading this chapter. She said, "Mom, from my perspective, I had repented. I had tried to make things right." In our pharisaical manner, we judged that she wasn't *really* repentant. We were trying to force her to be in complete agreement with our values.

As I look back now and see the minor thing that we overreacted to, I feel a bit embarrassed. You see, my daughter was not doing drugs. She was not pregnant. As an 18-year-old, she had chosen to hide the fact that she was dating a boy she had deep feelings for. She was in a web of lying, deceiving, and resisting our leadership.

We taught the "guard your heart" and no-dating principles in our home in such a strict way that our daughter felt like she couldn't be honest with her choice. Our teaching had moved from being grace-based and Spirit-led to being fault-finding and condemning. We had become like the Pharisees. We were holy and pure in our own eyes.

The Goodness of God Covers
Our Imperfections as Parents

If you are trying to live up to an image of what it looks like to be a perfect parent, you are setting yourself up for disappointment.

The only perfect parent is our Father in heaven. Although He was a perfect parent and He had provided a paradise for Adam and Eve to live in, they still chose to disobey Him.

As a human race, we chose to rebel against our perfect Father. Because of their sin nature, your children at some point or another will rebel against your leadership. They may be outwardly rebellious or inwardly rebellious. If you try to control them or put a legalistic structure in place, it may backfire on you. If you are presently dealing with a rebellious child, no matter if they are a toddler or a teenager, consider this course of action:

- *Humble yourself.*
- *Seek Godly counsel and partnership.*
- *Become a learner and gain new parenting skills.*
- *Admit your imperfections and mistakes.*
- *Be firm, steadfast, and consistent.*
- *Put your trust in the goodness of God.*
- *Gain new confidence that God will help you.*

Turning a Corner

Repentance is a radical heart change—turning completely away from sin and turning completely to God. Repentance is a total heart-mind turn-around. What's complicated about parenting is ultimately we are not the judge of what is completely right and wrong. The Ultimate Judge is our parent. Our loving Father in heaven is also the Awesome and Holy Ancient of Days. He is sinless.

We will stand shoulder to shoulder with our earthly children before our God one day. As an earthly mom I am also a sister in Christ to my children. God is able

> *Repentance is a total heart-mind turn-around.*

to see the intent of our hearts and the things that are hidden from our perspective. We may be "model parents" from earthly standards, but by God's standard we all fall short.

There were a few months when our relationship with our daughter was completely severed. Then one day I was driving down the road with our sons, and we saw Rachel driving beside us. I had Dre roll down the window, and I said, "Come home."

I didn't realize it at the time, but I needed to come home, too. I needed to come home to my Father in heaven. I needed to repent of my pharisaical ways and turn my perspective completely around.

A significant moment happened when Wayne and I met with our daughter and a counselor. It was not what the counselor said, but a picture that my husband had at the end of our time that stuck with me. He recalled a book that I had read to my daughter dozens of times called *The Wind and the Sun*.

In the story, the wind and the sun are having an argument about which one was the most powerful. The sun suggested a test to look down on the walking man bundled in a coat. Whichever could make the man take off his jacket would win the wager. The wind went first and began to blow as hard as he could. The harder he blew, the closer the man pulled his jacket. Worn out, he let the sun go next. The sun came out and shown brightly. The man rejoiced in the warmth of the sun and gladly took off his jacket.

As Wayne recalled the story of *The Wind and the Sun*, he sensed the simplicity of showing the warmth of God's goodness was the key to our daughter's heart. We had been so focused on what we felt was the "truth" of the situation that we had missed the greater truth of God's mercy.

"Speak and act as those who are going to be judged by the law that gives freedom, because judgment without mercy

our children close during a family vacation time, and I read my repentance letter to them, feeling broken by the weight of my own sin. My husband and I asked our children to forgive us, and we made a commitment to them to lead them, but not control them. We exhorted them to choose wisely.

The Pitfall of Manipulation and Control

One of the pitfalls that the enemy has designed for Christian parents is to trap them through their good intentions. Most of the time we don't see ourselves as being manipulating or controlling. We often just feel that we are "right," and we have the Bible to back-up our view. We feel strongly about the positive choices that we hope our children will make. We project our own idea of the best choice onto our adolescent and adult children. We fail to give them a chance to learn how to choose for themselves.

God is our safe place, and we need to create a sense of safety in our relationship with our children. They need to know they can come to us when they fail. Because sin was dealt with on the cross, we no longer need to be punished or controlled. In the New Covenant of God's grace we need to learn to manage our freedom responsibly.

> *God is our safe place, and we need to create a sense of safety in our relationship with our children.*

In *Loving Our Kids on Purpose*, author Danny Silk says, "When love and freedom replace punishment and fear as the motivating forces in the relationship between parent and child, the quality of life improves dramatically for all involved. They feel safe with each other, and the anxiety that created distance in the relationships is chased away by the sense of love, honor, and value for one another." (Danny Silk, *Loving Our Kids on Purpose*, page 43).

When our children learn to walk with God personally and intimately, they no longer need to be controlled from the outside. As Christians, they have the capability and responsibility to control themselves. As they become adults, they have the choice to obey God's Word in their own lives.

Build into the fabric of your home and heart the value of love and respect. Be willing to humbly assess how your actions are affecting your children emotionally. Often we excuse our *actions* because we know that we had a good intent of the heart. No matter how hard we try, we can't *make* our children obey God's ways from their heart. Only they can choose to embrace God's goodness personally.

WATCH
Watch the free video
Replacing My Manipulation with God's Goodness
at www.SueDetweiler.com.

A PRAYER FOR
Goodness

FATHER IN HEAVEN,
I COME AS YOUR CHILD.
I WANT TO LOVE LIKE YOU LOVE.
I WANT TO LEAD LIKE YOU LEAD.
FORGIVE ME FATHER, FOR I HAVE FALLEN SHORT.
SHOW ME MY OWN SIN THAT IS HIDDEN FROM MY EYES.
FATHER, YOU HAVE PLACED YOUR MOST VALUED TREASURE
IN MY HANDS - "MY" CHILDREN ARE FIRST YOUR CHILDREN.
I AM STEWARDING THEIR LIVES IN MY HANDS.
YOU HAVE NOT SET ME IN THIS TRUSTED PLACE
BECAUSE OF MY OWN EXPERTISE OR WISDOM.
I AM COMPLETELY DEPENDENT ON YOU TO LEAD ME.
YOUR WAYS ARE HIGHER THAN MY WAYS,
YOUR THOUGHTS ARE HIGHER THAN MY THOUGHTS.
I CHOOSE TO HUMBLE MYSELF BEFORE YOU.
HELP ME LEARN FROM MY MISTAKES
AND THE MISTAKES OF OTHERS.
I PUT MY CHILDREN IN YOUR HANDS.

Faithfulness

Faithfulness is unfailing love and fidelity.

It is unswerving loyalty.

Faithfulness is constant and steadfast.

Faithfulness is committed and dependable.

It is reliable, trustworthy, and devoted.

When faithfulness is close, it is authentic and true.

Faithfulness is beautiful and unchanging.

Faithfulness fights for you up until the end of the battle.

Faithfulness moves forward step by step.

Faithfulness is the power and motivation
for Christian living.

Chapter 8

REPLACING MY FEAR
WITH GOD'S FAITHFULNESS

I woke up with a smile on my face. "Wayne, you won't guess what I dreamt this time."

For six weeks I had the same type of dream. Every night I had another baby. One night it was twin toddler girls with dark hair. In the dream I am flabbergasted that I had *more* children. *Six is enough!* In my dream, I'm learning to know their names and embracing the fact that I am a mom again.

Another night it's a baby with reddish blond curls, and she is clinging to me in a bathroom stall, abandoned by her mother. I go to the front desk of the hotel and say, "Whose baby is this?"

The concierge looks at her computer screen and back up at me, "She is your baby, ma'am."

"What? Another baby!" As six weeks went by, night after night I had a different child. All the children were of different ages, genders, and races.

At every major change or transition in my life, I have dreams of babies. In this particular season in life, we had been at our present congregation for seventeen years. For most of those years, we had both been serving as associate pastors.

"What did you dream this time?" Wayne asked.

"This time I was a mother engorged with breast milk. The milk from my breast was dripping to the ground. I jumped into my car and sped toward my children…" Any nursing mother of a newborn knows the urgency a mom feels to get to her child in this situation.

We quietly pondered the dream. "Wayne, I think God is trying to get our attention. Change is coming."

My husband was silent. He had already been forced into a change that none of us wanted. He was just waiting for me to catch up with him.

My husband had been quietly laid off from the job he held as an associate pastor. Since it was not announced on a Sunday morning, most people didn't know. We still sat on the front row. I was often on the platform, and we were still at all the functions. People assumed Wayne was still on staff and would often call him with their needs.

Wayne was invited to stay as a volunteer pastoral team member while I kept my same position as an associate pastor. Our monthly income was cut in half. We still had six children, who were at the most expensive times of their lives. I felt a tremendous amount of pressure as the main bread-winner.

I also felt torn. As a mom, I had an ideal job. Our senior pastor was a champion for women using their gifts in public ministry and keeping their family a priority. I was able to work from my home on most days where I homeschooled all of my children. I served as the principal of the homeschool academy that my children attended. Not only was I able to be at my children's events, I often led them. I also had the privilege of overseeing an award-winning school of ministry for adults. I led two different schools, two different faculties, and two different administrative teams. I loved the challenge. Even more, I loved the people.

I kept pondering the possible symbolic meaning of my dreams about babies. The season was changing. The girls had graduated from the academy and moved on. The boys were there, but with their special needs, they needed a different type of education. My husband was beginning a non-profit ministry called Life-Bridges. God was awakening in me a desire to minister globally as an author and speaker. Everything was indeed changing.

After going through an intense day of meetings, I sat in my colleague's office. I told him about my recurring baby dreams. He asked, "Have you asked God whether it is time for you to transition out of your role here?"

"No." I hadn't asked that question. *Why hadn't I asked that question?*

Then I knew the answer—fear. It was fear of the unknown; fear of failure, rejection, financial lack, starting all over. It was even fear of God not showing up. I felt terrified that we wouldn't have any money coming in.

Here I was, a strong, confident woman cowering from change. I was hiding in what was good. I loved walking into the kindergarten class at the academy and having all the kids surround me and hug me as their principal. I loved the amazing people I worked with for so many years. We had history together. I loved the birthday parties, weddings, and baby showers. I loved the community of friends. I was afraid of losing everything.

Fear Comes in All Shapes and Sizes

Fear is one of the most negative human emotions with many forms: anxiety, dread, doubt, uncertainty, and insecurity, just to name a few. Sometimes fear shows up in a racing heart and sweaty palms when you think a burglar is in the house. Other times, fear is hidden in caution—because it's only a figment of our imaginations, of what *could* happen.

When does fear plague you the most? Does fear attack you in the middle of the night when you are all alone? Does fear sneak up on you in a crowd of people? Everyone experiences fear. Sometimes it means waking up to your worst fears, like when I woke up in the middle of a house fire.

Fear is no respecter of age or gender or position in life. If you spend your life trying to avoid fear, you won't be able to live. Fear is an unpleasant emotion for everyone. It may be caused by the belief that you are going to experience physical or emotional pain. You may have mixed feelings of dread or anxiety. You may be fearful of heights. There are phobias of all kinds of things.

When fear is a prevalent emotion in your home, your children learn to walk on eggshells. They will sense your anxiousness, doubt, or dread.

Fear can paralyze you from attempting to do what you feel called to. Fear stunts your growth and denies you God's promised inheritance.

> *Other times, fear is hidden in caution – because it's only a figment of our imaginations, of what could happen.*

Surrender Yourself to God—Trust in His Faithfulness

I wouldn't have admitted to you or myself that I was paralyzed by fear from moving forward. I just found myself dreaming at night.

Alone in my sleep, I could admit that it was time to move into a new season. It was time to face my fears and follow God's promptings.

After my colleague challenged me to ask God about whether we were being called into a new season, I came home and wrote in my prayer journal:

"Lord God, you know how fearful I am. I desperately want Your will. In Your name, Jesus, I ask you to fill me with faith even to write this journal entry. I don't want to make a mistake. If I am honest with You, I'm afraid of failure…

By faith, I am surrendering myself to You. I will go anywhere You want me to go. I will say anything You want me to say. I will do anything You want me to do. I trust You."

As I surrendered to God, I felt His peace flood my heart. I began to remember His faithfulness in leading and guiding Wayne and I through difficult transitions.

A few months later we had our senior pastor and his wife over and washed their feet. As we knelt down before them, we shared our love for them and thanked them for all the years we had serving together. We also asked them to release us. We had a wonderful conversation, sensing God's presence in the room.

The next week we were surprised by an opportunity for Wayne to serve as a senior assistant pastor at a primarily African-American church. We laughed at God's faithfulness to provide us a way for Wayne to serve the church and for me to write, speak, and work with the non-profit ministry.

I share these details, because at the beginning of any journey we will often experience the fear of the unknown. As we walk with God, He makes all things possible in His time. Sometimes we walk forward afraid, but look back at His faithfulness.

By completing this book, I am entering into a new season in my life. Eighteen years ago when my father was dying, he encouraged

me to write this book. He laid his
hands on my belly (I was pregnant
with Sarah), and he prayed for
God's favor. He encouraged me to
fulfill the mission that God had
created me for.

When I began this adventure
into the unknown, I didn't know
what I was doing. I am still
holding tightly to God, trusting
in His faithfulness.

Our journey is never just about ourselves. Our journey is about others.

I have discovered a miraculous gift—contentment. I am more
content than at any time in my life. I wake up consistently joyful,
ready to inspire women on their adventures of faith.

Our journey is never just about ourselves. Our journey is about
others. We encourage others with the courage we receive from God.

Put Yourself in God's Story

As a mom, you likely laid down things you were passionate
about in order to raise your children. You may have made sacrifices
so that you could be home with them. You may have needed to be a
working mom. If time has passed, are you in a new season, too?

*Ask yourself this question: If I could do anything in the world,
and I knew that I couldn't fail and that I had plenty of money, what
would I do?*

Your unique answer to the above question reveals your passions
and dreams. God has made you with a destiny. Part of that destiny
is to be a mom. Have you noticed that even your role as a mom is
constantly changing? The school bus pulls up to your door, they get
in, and you have time you hadn't had in years. The next thing you
know, there are so many cars in the driveway, you no longer need to

drive them everywhere because they now drive their own cars. Next, they leave for college, the mission field, or they get married.

In this life, everything changes. As soon as you think you master one stage of motherhood, you have transitioned into the next season.

God's faithfulness endures every change that life could bring. His faithfulness is what helps you to be faithful to your children at every season of their lives.

Do It Afraid

When you are tempted to get stuck in your past because of fear, follow my example. Do it afraid!

Every time I take a step forward out of obedience to God's call on my life, the step itself is a shot of confidence. No one is courageous in his own strength. True courage comes from God.

Face your fear and overcome it with God's faithfulness. Your example of being a fearless woman will encourage your children to take faith-filled steps in their lives.

I know if you are reading this book with a beautiful headshot of me on the cover, you could still think: *Sue has it all together. She has a husband and six children. Her life looks perfect.*

Come look into the window of my life. I have no make-up on my face. I am sitting in sweats and have slippers on my feet. My husband and I had an argument this morning. (Of course, it was my fault. I was too bossy). I have dishes sitting in my sink from my many children moving through the house headed to school and work. We have bills, and Wayne's role as an assistant pastor came to an end recently. We are now making our

> *Face your fear and overcome it with God's faithfulness.*

home at Cross Point Community Church and starting all over with building relationships.

You would think that with Wayne's most recent job transition I would be even more afraid than when I first got out of the boat and began walking on the water (See John 6:15-21). As I keep my eyes on Jesus, my feet don't sink into the waves of the storm. In the midst of the storm you will be transformed.

> *Because He laid down His life, I am able to lay down my life for my children.*

I am transformed. I am fearless. The things that used to frighten me no longer cause me anxiety. The only thing I can point to is God's faithfulness.

My life is not perfect. God is perfect. My story is important because it is His story being lived out in the frailty of human flesh. It is His Spirit alive in me that makes it possible for me to walk in His faithfulness. Because He laid down His life, I am able to lay down my life for my children.

Facing your fear will free you to see God's faithfulness. Shake yourself awake. Shake off your excuses. Face your fear. Do what God is calling you to. Do it afraid, if necessary. Just get moving. He takes the mess of your life and weaves His message into it.

Overcome Fear with His Faithfulness

Jesus did not promise us that we would have no fear in this life. Rather, He challenged us to take heart and overcome our fear with faith. Jesus said that we would experience trials and stress. We are able to overcome because He overcame. Jesus said,

"These things I have spoken to you, that in Me you may have peace.
In the world you will have tribulation; but be of good cheer,
I have overcome the world."
John 16:33, NKJV

As a mom, the way to replace your fear is to embrace God's faithfulness through the power of the Holy Spirit. Your life is not based on what you can do in your own strength. It is not based on what you can accomplish. In this world you will face fear, but you don't have to face it alone. You have the power of the Holy Spirit to clothe you with wisdom, direction, and boldness.

Time after time in my own dark hour of my soul, when life looks pitch black, a hymn of hope will rise up in my heart and come out of my mouth in the song, "Great is Thy Faithfulness."

God sees me in the middle of the night, tears dripping down my face, quietly singing, "Great is Thy Faithfulness." He hears me in the morning light standing with my face lifted to heaven singing, "Great is Thy Faithfulness." He intimately connects with me as I load the dishwasher and wipe the counters singing in my heart, "Great is Thy Faithfulness."

God's faithfulness penetrates the cold death-like grip of fear. His faithfulness transforms perspective. His faithfulness shoots courage into my veins making it possible to more than just survive a dreaded day.

In this world you will face terrible things. You will experience excruciating pain. Fear is a given in this world. The final promise of eternity will outlast all of our fears:

"He will wipe every tear from their eyes, and there
will be no more death or sorrow or crying or
pain. All these things are gone forever."
Revelation 21:4, NLT

God is so faithful that He doesn't delegate to the angels the task of cheering people up. He is the One who comes and personally wipes our tears. Think of the tenderness of that moment. God is the only One who truly understands your pain. Others will empathize with some of it. It is God who made a plan to take away your death, sorrow, and crying *forever*.

As a mom, know that when you are fearful, He is faithful.

WATCH
Watch the free video
Replacing My Fear with God's Faithfulness
at www.SueDetweiler.com.

A PRAYER FOR
Faithfulness

—⊷⊷⊷—

FAITHFUL, EVERLASTING GOD,
YOU ARE THE ONE THAT I OPEN MY HEART TO.
ALL THAT I AM I PLACE INTO YOUR CARING HANDS.
YOUR FAITHFULNESS REACHES TO THE HEAVENS.
I WILL SING OF WHO YOU ARE TO ALL THE GENERATIONS.
YOU ARE FOREVER STEADFAST AND ALWAYS PRESENT.
I GIVE MYSELF TO YOU TODAY AND EVERY DAY.
I WANT TO WALK WITH YOU EVERY MOMENT.
I WANT TO BE LIKE YOU.
LET YOUR LOVE AND MERCY
COVER ME TODAY AS I POUR MYSELF OUT BEFORE YOU.
USE ME TO SELFLESSLY SHARE WITH MY CHILD YOUR LOVE.
EVERYTHING I AM I GIVE TO YOU.
YOU HAVE BEEN FAITHFUL TO ME, AND
I PLEDGE TO BE FAITHFUL TO YOU.
LET YOUR FAITHFUL LOVE FLOW THROUGH ME,
WARMING OUR HOME WITH YOUR PRESENCE.
I TRUST YOU COMPLETELY.
I PRAY IN YOUR NAME,
AMEN.

—⊷⊷⊷—

Gentleness

Gentleness is kind and understanding.
Gentleness is a tender love.
It is chivalrous and noble.
Gentleness is strength in Restraint
Gentleness is a calming influence.
Gentleness is considerate and always benevolent.
It is good-natured.
Gentleness is mild, sweet, and merciful.
It is easy to be around.
Gentleness is comfortable,
sympathetic, and compassionate.
It is wise with foresight, and
strong with dignity.
It abides in the power of God.
Gentleness strengthens the weak.
Gentleness is healing for the sick.
It is caring for the poor.
The gentleness of God is the
Fruit of His Holy Spirit.

Chapter 9

REPLACING MY PRIDE
WITH GOD'S GENTLENESS

Arguing with my husband, I heard the Holy Spirit say, "*Not another word!*" But I had four more words that would prove my point.

Those four words were the gasoline that enflamed our disagreement. Now we were facing a full-blown war. My humble husband went for a drive rather than retaliate. It gave me time to think, and the Holy Spirit room to convict my heart.

Why do I always think I am right?

The answer to that question was really quite simple. I had the audacity to think I was right 100 percent of the time, because I was walking in pride. Pride puffs up. Pride deceives. Pride is rooted in self. Pride negatively impacts every relationship in our lives. Pride separates us from intimacy with God and with others. If we continue to walk in pride we will be very lonely.

Pride has reared its ugly head in so many ways in my life as a mom. One of my deepest regrets is blaming my children for things that were not their fault. I deceived myself that I was just holding them accountable. Pointing the finger is never helpful. Blame-shifting does not build responsible children.

You know what life is like. On a daily basis things happen. The milk is spilt on the counter. The dishes are not stacked. The bathroom is not cleaned. Someone forgets a school assignment. The dog is not fed. The list is endless with potential things that can go wrong in a household.

Pride hates to be inconvenienced. So rather than being gentle and understanding, pride demands that someone accept responsibility for the mistake that someone else made. Pride always justifies its own actions. Pride looks at self with "pure intentions of the heart" but scrutinizes the actions of others.

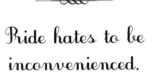

Pride hates to be inconvenienced.

Pride agrees with itself. Pride often has bed partners. Pride provides detailed examples of why and how it is right. Pride exonerates itself but keeps a long list of recorded wrongs of another.

Pride dresses in all kinds of clothing. Pride can look loud and brash with a feathered headdress to capture everyone's attention.

The most deadly and devious pride hides under religious piety. The Scripture warns against this.

> *"Everyone proud and arrogant in heart is disgusting,*
> *hateful, and exceedingly offensive to the Lord; be assured*
> *[I pledge it] they will not go unpunished."*
> Proverbs 16:5, AMP

This is the kind of pride Jesus confronted in the Pharisees. One day Jesus was speaking and the teachers and Pharisees brought a woman who had been caught in the act of adultery. They showed their bias against women by neglecting to bring the man who was also caught in the act.

They shoved the woman in front of the crowd to make an example of her crime and to trap Jesus.

> *"'Teacher,' they said to Jesus, 'this woman was caught in the*
> *act of adultery. The law of Moses says to stone her. What do you say?'*
> *They were trying to trap him into saying something*
> *they could use against him, but Jesus stooped down and*
> *wrote in the dust with his finger. They kept demanding an answer,*
> *so he stood up again and said, 'All right, but let the one who has*
> *never sinned throw the first stone!' Then he stooped down*
> *again and wrote in the dust. When the accusers heard this,*
> *they slipped away one by one, beginning with the oldest,*
> *until only Jesus was left in the middle of the crowd*
> *with the woman. Then Jesus stood up again and said to*
> *the woman, 'Where are your accusers?*
> *Didn't even one of them condemn you?'*
> *'No, Lord,' she said.*
> *And Jesus said, 'Neither do I. Go and sin no more.'"*
> John 8:3-11, NLT

Jesus could not be trapped by religious pride. He responded in compassion and truth at the same time. His response shows that He walked in a spirit of gentleness at all times. He cared more about the woman than proving a religious point or preserving His reputation.

One of the most painful things to deal with, as a mom, is the choices of our children to sin. When they are younger, it is easier to discipline them and try to help them see how their choices lack love. However, when they are older and sin is covered up in its own deceptive clothing, the Holy Spirit needs to reveal it to them. Jesus was able to care for the woman, not condemn her, and say, "Go and sin no more." With our children, we want to be like Jesus to them.

You Can Be "Right" But All "Wrong"

It's more important for you to be in right relationship with others than to try to always be right. Admit when you are wrong. It will go a long way toward healing your relationships. Love keeps no record of wrongs (See 1 Corinthians 13:5). Pride not only records wrong, it never forgets a wrong. Pride rehearses mistakes over and over again. Even if you have apologized and tried to change your ways, pride's evil taskmaster exaggerates sin's claims and never forgives a wrong.

Admit when you are wrong. It will go a long way toward healing your relationships.

Pride justifies itself. Pride never has to say, "I'm sorry." Pride isn't sorry. Pride thinks only through the eyes of self. God calls us to walk in holiness in our relationships. This doesn't mean that every relationship will be reconciled this side of heaven. Holiness means we will pick up the phone and make things right when we can. It means we will get dressed daily in gentleness and humility.

"Since God chose you to be the holy people he loves, you must clothe yourselves with tenderhearted mercy, kindness, humility, gentleness, and patience. Make allowance for each other's faults, and forgive anyone who offends you. Remember, the Lord forgave you, so you must forgive others. Above all, clothe yourselves with love, which binds us all together in perfect harmony.

And let the peace that comes from Christ rule in your hearts.
For as members of one body you are called to live in peace.
And always be thankful."
Colossians 3:12-15, NLT

Clothed In a Spirit of Gentleness

My husband gets dressed every day in clothing of gentleness. His strength under restraint has been one of the qualities that has made him such a good father to our four daughters and now two sons with special needs. I was drawn to Wayne's gentleness when I first met him. My Grandma Burkholder, who was in her nineties, wanted to know about *this pastor* who was engaged to her granddaughter. I said, "Grandma, I can trust him. He is gentle and kind."

Gentleness can sometimes be underrated in our culture. One morning I was leading early morning prayer at church. I arrived earlier than the others, so I began to pray for each leader to walk in the power and the fruit of the Holy Spirit. I mentioned each trait that represents the Holy Spirit: love, joy, peace, patience, kindness, goodness, faithfulness... And then when I got to gentleness I had a revelation. *God Himself is gentle.*

I remembered King David's words about God when he said, "Your gentleness has made me great." (Psalm 18:35, NKJV). David had boasted about God's awesome power, and then he made it personal. The God who "flew upon the wings of the wind" (See Psalm 18:10, NKJV) also gently positioned David for greatness.

God's gentleness finds expression when a mom embraces her role to be a nurturing force in her home. Just as a mom tenderly carries her newborn baby, she needs to continue to gently protect her adult son's and daughter's hearts.

Oh, how many mistakes I have made in my desire to train my children in holiness. A mom becomes a Pharisee when it is more important for her child to maintain a religious code of ethics than to honestly express themselves. With my older children, I confronted rebellion too harshly. What I failed to see is that any overly harsh parent can actually drive a child to rebel.

Jesus was approachable for those who recognized their brokenness. The woman who came carrying an alabaster flask may have been in the crowd when Jesus said, "Do not judge others, and you will not be judged. Do not condemn others, or it will all come back against you. Forgive others, and you will be forgiven." (Luke 6:37, NLT)

This woman knew Jesus was safe. She was confident she would not be rejected. She watched His actions. She saw how He treated the woman caught in adultery. So the woman came carrying her alabaster flask, holding the most precious hope in her hands, her costly dowry. She poured it out with abandonment.

The woman loved much because she had been forgiven much. Her sin was cleansed. With her tears that flowed with thankfulness, she washed Jesus' feet. Her unbound hair reflected the new freedom found in her relationship with Jesus.

> "When a certain immoral woman from that city heard
> he was eating there, she brought a beautiful alabaster jar filled
> with expensive perfume. Then she knelt behind him at his feet,
> weeping. Her tears fell on his feet, and she wiped them off with
> her hair. Then she kept kissing his feet and putting perfume
> on them. When the Pharisee who had invited him saw this,
> he said to himself, 'If this man were a prophet, he would know
> what kind of woman is touching him. She's a sinner!'
> Then Jesus answered his thoughts. 'Simon,' he said to the
> Pharisee, 'I have something to say to you.'
> 'Go ahead, Teacher,' Simon replied. Then Jesus told him

this story: 'A man loaned money to two people—500 pieces of
silver to one and 50 pieces to the other. But neither of them
could repay him, so he kindly forgave them both, canceling their debts.
Who do you suppose loved him more after that?'
Simon answered, 'I suppose the one for whom
he canceled the larger debt.' 'That's right,' Jesus said."
Luke 7:37-43, NLT

Jesus then compared Simon to the woman. It was customary to offer water to the guest to wash the dust from the road off his feet. Simon had snubbed Jesus and neglected to offer this courtesy. It was polite to greet with a kiss, but Simon was too proud to greet Jesus in this manner. Nor did he anoint His head with oil.

The woman, on the other hand, washed the dust from Jesus' feet with her tears. Then, she dried Jesus' feet with her hair. She kissed Jesus' feet with tenderness and anointed His feet with her perfume.

The woman came to Simon's home with many sins. She left his home completely forgiven. She loved Jesus much and was forgiven much. Her faith saved her, and she went in God's peace.

Jesus was unconcerned about His reputation. Simon, on the other hand, was completely offended that this woman made her way into his home. He judged and condemned her without even knowing her. His pride kept him from welcoming the woman in her brokenness.

Are Your Children Able
to Come to You in Brokenness?

Do your children know that you will receive them and welcome them when they make mistakes? Are you able to meet them with truth and mercy at the same time? Do you respond to them like Jesus, or do you respond like Simon, the Pharisee? There will be plenty of Pharisees in your life to condemn you and your children. Make your home a safe place of refuge.

Raising children in Nashville, the city that is often called the buckle of the Bible Belt, can be challenging. The white picket fences of suburbia where everyone goes to church (or lies about it) can hide a religious duplicity. Children learn to be well-mannered with smiles on their faces and "Yes ma'am" on their lips. They learn the skill of flying under the radar rather than truly being honest.

Religious legalism hinders real relationship with your children. No matter how young or old your children are, develop a home of safety and transparency. Your children can sense if you are more concerned about your reputation than being open to their needs and concerns. They know if they can open up to you, or if you will automatically judge and condemn them.

Hopefully, you have this place of trust and safety with all of your children. They know that if they open up to you, you will not judge them or condemn them. You will not be overly worried about your reputation because of their sin. You will be able to be like Jesus—compassionate and truthful at the same time.

Lead them to Jesus. They need to experience Him. He is the truth that will set them free. They need a personal, intimate encounter with Jesus, who accepts them as they come. Even if you are a teacher-preacher, your children will just shut you out if you preach at them. No matter how much truth comes out of your mouth, they need to experience Jesus as the truth.

They need a personal, intimate encounter with Jesus, who accepts them as they come.

*"And you will **know** the truth, and the truth will set you free."*
John 8:32, NLT

We can only know the truth by personally experiencing Jesus. We perceive truth when we understand and recognize God's ways. We only come to know His ways when we abide with Him. For it is the "goodness of God that leads you to repentance." (Romans 2:4, NKJV).

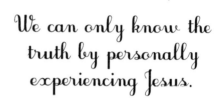

We can only know the truth by personally experiencing Jesus.

Pride Can Hinder You
From Accurately Seeing Your Child

Just like Simon, the Pharisee, did not accurately perceive the heart behind the woman with the alabaster flask, pride can prevent you from accurately seeing your child.

If your child has drawn breath outside your womb, they have already made mistakes. If you have a number of children, they will make different types of mistakes. Develop a sense of humor to combat magnifying their mistakes. If you make a big thing about something small, they may be afraid to bring the serious things to you.

God's Gentleness is
Shown Through Humble Hearts

Humble yourself before your children. If you consistently walk in transparency about your own mistakes, you will pave the way for your children to be transparent. Knowing your authority as a parent does not mean you need to act like you have it all together. Your kids are keenly aware of your mistakes and inconsistencies.

When my children were small, I tried to acknowledge times when I made a mistake as their mom. I would put myself in the "time out chair." They would come and place their tiny hands on me and "pray for Mommy." Taking that moment to let the innocence of their voices rise in prayer gave the breath of the Holy Spirit room to convict me of my own need for Him.

One of the most precious times with my earthly father came when he humbled himself to my husband and me. My dad was a hardworking man with a warm heart. He always meant well. At 30 years of age I had never heard him apologize. On New Year's Eve he said some hurtful things to me that I knew he didn't mean. I found myself crying myself to sleep.

The next day my father said, "I'm sorry for how I acted." It was a simple act, but it had a profound impact on our relationship. We were reconciled at the heart. From that time on, our relationship became more mature.

My father did not go back and "own" all the things I probably thought were his fault at the time. How blind I was. I was the one acting in pride. He, as the father, took the first step of humility. I took the next step and received it.

I am so thankful I did. At the time, there was no way to know that it would be only a few short years till his early death. Oh, how valuable those years were with my father. He was the first one who encouraged me to write this book. He told me I was a writer and I needed to develop my skill.

My father spent time with my husband and me and delighted in our growing family. Oh, how I wish he could be here for my sons. Since he is in the great cloud of witnesses cheering us on, I know he is also laughing at Ezequiel's antics and smiling at Dre's journey to manhood (See Hebrews 12:1-2).

Every Moment Counts

Our time with our children is so short. It should be treasured and holy before God. We can't afford to be proud or arrogant with them. As mothers, we need the tender gentleness of Jesus that wipes away every tear and binds up every wound. He cares for the weak.

"He will not crush the weakest reed or put out a flickering candle.
He will bring justice to all who have been wronged."
Isaiah 42:3, NLT

God is the One who knows what is just. As moms we may think we have eyes in the back of our heads, but we don't. God is the One who sees. He sees us when we have been harsh with our children.

As a mom you are to be a nurturing force for your children. Yes, you need to instruct them in right and wrong. But let Jesus be your model for motherhood. He never condoned the sin. Neither did He reject the sinner. The only ones He was hard on were those who were self-righteous, religious, and proud.

Guard your home against pharisaical rituals. Surround your home with the joyful exuberance of freely walking with God. Let your children experience God Himself. Make His presence attractive in your home.

As you replace your own pride with God's gentleness, you depend daily on God's wisdom to guide you. The truth is, you don't have it figured out. Most of the time you don't know what to do. As you rest in the humble, forgiving embrace of love, you will represent God's goodness to your child.

WATCH
Watch the free video
Replacing My Pride with God's Gentleness
at www.SueDetweiler.com.

A PRAYER FOR
Gentleness

Love of my Life,
I want to dance with You.
I am so sorry for the times that I have
resisted your leading and guiding in my life.
I have stepped on your toes and tried to lead you.
Your embrace is so gentle, firm, and strong.
You know my weaknesses.
You dance with me and make me beautiful,
spinning me around, holding me close,
smiling in my eyes, whispering in my ear.
I want you to dance with my child
like you dance with me.
I will no longer be the harsh dance instructor.
I will no longer correct them or shame them,
worried about how I will look as their mom.
Rather, I will put their hands in Yours.
I want you to be the first Lover in my child's life.
Whisper sweetness in her ear.
Congratulate his strength.
Your gentleness will make my child great.

 Download written prayers at **www.SueDetweiler.com.**

Self-Control

Self-control is composure of mind,
body, and spirit.
It is the restraint of selfish cravings.
Gentleness is temperate behavior.
Self-discipline and serenity are her sisters.
Self-control brings poise and presence of mind to choose wisely.
It is calm self-possession with a
spirit-inspired will power.
Self-control is the ability to control emotions,
behaviors, and desires to
obtain the long-term reward.
It avoids destructive impulses.
It embraces healthy habits.
Self-control grants focus on eternal benefits.
It overcomes temptation.
Self-control brings a hunger for God
that embraces the eternal
and His purposes.

Chapter 10
REPLACING MY SELF-INDULGENCE
WITH GOD'S SELF-CONTROL

Some of my earliest memories involve sneaking food and candy alone in my bedroom. Celebrating by crunching on Pringles®, Smarties®, and Snickers®, and eating chocolate chip cookies late at night in the kitchen with the lights out so no one would notice.

When I was older, although much more aware of needing to eat healthy foods, I would deceive myself by gorging on salads topped with cheese, croutons, and creamy dressing. At holiday gatherings I would overeat by devouring ham, green beans, and baked potatoes soaked in butter and sour cream.

I was able to hide my obsession with food by the vicious cycle of overeating then dieting—until I became pregnant with my first child. My whole body, not just my belly, swelled to over 200 pounds on my 5'4" frame. I had a problem.

I could feel the magnetic pull of a giant black hole that my many obese ancestors had fallen into. I knew if I didn't get help, I would likely be overweight for the rest of my life.

By the grace of God, I was able to manage my weight most of my life by becoming a member of Weight Watchers® and the YMCA. I successfully lost the weight after every baby, proudly marching around with my tiny waist after four pregnancies.

As a mom I have taken my children on a roller coaster ride concerning self-indulgence and self-sacrifice. They have witnessed my adulterous love affair with food.

Yes, I know that overindulgence is not just about food, but that is the drug of choice for the majority of Christian women I know. Yes, there are shopaholics, alcoholics, and workaholics, too. There are women who suffer with addictions to drugs, nicotine, and sex.

For the sake of being transparent and honest, I will talk about my addiction to sugar and savory foods. As you are reading this chapter, your own vices will likely come to the surface.

On a daily basis, I carefully kept record of what I ate and measured the amount of exercise I was getting. But at holidays and special events, I would binge. I remember holding Sarah's hand walking through the grocery store looking for a treat to celebrate the girls being out of school.

Everyone in my house knew about my love-hate relationship with food. After the holidays, the strict Momma Health Nazi came back to the surface. My sons came from Brazil, and one of the questions they learned to ask in English was, "Is this healthy?" Of course, they had heard this from me.

Everything was going well as I proudly tracked my progress of success. I measured my heart rate when I ran. I measured the grams of protein I ate every day. I was the model of success, until I encountered a perfect storm of adverse factors that impacted my weight gain.

As I write this book, this is the second time in my life I have been overweight. Just like when I was pregnant with my first child and could no longer hide my food addiction, I am facing this giant once again. Thank goodness your headshot does not show your backside.

Over the last five years, with increased stress, physical injury, hormonal changes, autoimmune disease, metabolic issues, bacterial infections, and other things you don't want to hear about, I have gained unwanted weight. Yes, I can point to all of these things that threw me off-kilter as causing my weight gain, but really I would not be in this situation if I did not have a love affair with food.

Has my over-indulgent sin affected my children? You bet it has. They are so sick of hearing me talk about my health needs. They have seen my patterns of inconsistency all of their lives.

The re-emergence of the physical impact of the sin of overindulgence came to the forefront of our family's attention a couple of years ago. After Thanksgiving I spent the entire next week in bed, so sick I couldn't get up. The week after Christmas of the same year, again, I became so sick I couldn't get out of bed.

My middle-aged body could no longer handle the overindulgent pattern of overeating. I was on the road to eating myself to death, just like my father who died at the early age of 62.

Why am I sharing this transparently in this book? Because I know that only by being truly honest, can both you and I gain greater victory and freedom. Our hope is in total surrender to God.

> God wants to be first in our lives. Everything that happens to us is sifted through His hands of love.

God wants to be first in our lives. Everything that happens to us is sifted through His hands of love. He could have prevented the physical challenges that ravaged my body. However, He will not override the gift that He has given each one of us—free choice.

Self-Control is our opportunity to freely choose to make God the first love of our life. Self-Control is our opportunity to deny ourselves and choose what our heart really craves—God.

As I re-establish self-control in this area and overcome my physical lust, God will be glorified. I also know that my personal victory in this area will pave the way for my children to overcome it as well.

Oh, how I wish my father had won this battle. How his wise words and generosity would have influenced the lives of my children. One of his dying regrets confessed to my ears was that he had not conquered this area of overeating in his life. He died of a cancer that may have been prevented if he had lived a life of self-control.

Our choices are life and death. To be a Life-Giving Mom we need to be alive.

What does your soul crave? What situations in your life have uncovered the hidden habits of your own heart? Don't be surprised if these hidden habits come to the surface. Embrace the opportunity to find greater freedom.

Become a victor, rather than a victim. Pass on to your children the warrior mentality. Be a warring mom that fights for life.

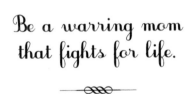

It's the Little Things

Overindulgence is a tricky habit to overcome because it hides in the wrapper of a "treat." In our culture a treat is not something that comes around once a year. Treats are demanded daily. As a mom you have a two-fold temptation—to overindulge yourself and your children.

God created each one of us in His image. He could have controlled us by His hand and given us perfect robotic lives. He chose instead to give us choice. His desire is that our greatest longing would be for Him. Anything or anyone who comes before this intimate relationship is an idol.

As a Life-Giving Mom I need to get honest with myself and ask the tough questions:

- What over-indulgent habits are causing death, not life?
- Who is my comforter?
- What is my reward?
- Who or what do I turn to in times of stress, anguish, or even delight?

Close your eyes and think about the truthful answers to the above questions.

When I closed my eyes, I thought of food. Wow. How embarrassing to admit. Food, something so temporal that is gone with a bite, rather than the eternal One who saved my soul. *Sigh.* Let me ask you the same raw questions again:

- What do you rely on more than you rely on God?
- What do you turn to when your day is going really bad or really good?
- Who is your secret lover?

Whatever your honest answer is, God is the only One worthy of holding that intimate place in your life.

Overindulgence Constructs
Secret Lovers that Never Satisfy

Food is just one of many illicit lovers women fall prey to. Maybe you *love* the cowboy boots with the pointy toes, so you pull out your credit card to charge just one more thing, even though your debt is spiraling out of control. You may want to be a good mother, but you love your romance novels so much that you don't get enough sleep at night and wake up cranky in the morning. You might turn to alcohol or cigarettes to calm your nerves after a tough day. You might find more sizzle in other idols that calm your nerves and comfort your soul.

Whatever your drug of choice, it isn't God Himself. When you overindulge yourself, you are setting yourself up for a life of being controlled by a substance rather than being self-controlled by the power of the Holy Spirit. You have a choice. You can change. It comes through your surrender to God and His ways.

With all of these health factors that have led to weight gain in my life, I have to get really honest and admit that the biggest reason that my weight has stayed on my body is an overindulgent love affair with food.

My transparent translation of 1 Corinthians 13:4-8 could be:

Food is patient and kind.
Butter is not jealous or boastful or proud or rude.
Sugar usually does demand its own way.
It makes me irritable, and it keeps a record of
wrong on the scales of life…
Food never gives up, never loses its flavor,
is always beckoning me to eat more.
Through every circumstance candy fails to bring me real
comfort, but I try again just in case it will work this time.

Of course, our heads know that God is love (not food). Our souls long for a tangible lover to take away our pain. Our own habits

> Our souls long for a tangible lover to take away our pain.

of overindulgence as a parent will often lead to similar patterns of overindulgence for our children.

Overindulgence Corrupts
Our Children's Cravings

My unhealthy desire for food began during the holidays when my father shoved peanut M&M'S® in our outstretched hands. He laughed and called himself the "Candy Man." My father tended to be a workaholic, and I desired his attention. Here, he was present and jolly during the holidays.

Is it any surprise that most of the time I maintain a healthy diet, and the times I overeat are during special events? When my body was healthy, I could exercise and hide the holiday splurges. The problem with patterns of overindulgence is that you can't hide them forever. Even our bodies develop things like "insulin resistance" because it can no longer keep up with our patterns of overindulgence.

Lust is trying to fill our legitimate need in illegitimate ways. The problem is that our soul has a hole in it only God can fill. Have you ever noticed that you are never satisfied with what lust demands? Someone addicted to cocaine can never get enough unless they go "cold turkey."

Alcoholics need to live with the fact that they are not able to have "just one drink." Food-aholics need to admit that there are probably some "trigger foods" that they may need to do without until heaven's banquet.

> *Lust is trying to fill our legitimate need in illegitimate ways.*

In the last thirty years, childhood obesity has doubled, and adolescent obesity has tripled. Being overweight in America is a growing epidemic. Moms foster this obesity every time they drive through a fast-food window and "super-size" their order of fries.

Americans' overindulgence is also seen in the national debt, which is rising every day. We teach our children to overspend every time we put Christmas on credit, or splurge for a dress we can't afford. The idols of our hearts are magnified in the hearts of our children. Our cravings become their entitlements.

Yesterday, I heard a child manipulate one of her parents through tearful protests. The father already treated his child to Dunkin' Donuts® and wisely decided they didn't need any more treats. In a loud protest the 9-year-old said, "You promised we would go to Cold Stone Creamery®. I have been looking forward to it all day! You promised!" I heard the dad laughingly say, "Okay, I did promise. We will go."

Our children have been overpromised and overindulged day after day. Unless there is a change of heart, this pretty little 9-year-old will grow into an ungrateful teenager, and eventually a discontent mom who overindulges her own manipulative children. Lord help us.

Every time we overindulge we put our short-term desires first, often short-circuiting our long-term objectives. Self-indulgence means feeding on the world rather than feasting on God, and it always has a price tag. Often, our empty feelings of discontent can drive us to addictive behaviors, which can lead to death.

Overindulgence Fuels Addiction

Addiction never satisfies. An addict always longs for more. Imelda Marcos is most well known for the 2,700 pairs of shoes that were left in the Manila Palace when she and her husband, Ferdinand, fled the country. The people of Manila went barefoot, while Imelda's insatiable desire for shoes marked her life. The enemy knows how to hook people with what may seem small or insignificant.

Addiction is a continuous repetition of a behavior even though it has adverse consequences. The problem of an addiction is that it is *never* fulfilled through indulgence. Addiction is an endless pit whose source of magnetic pull is hell.

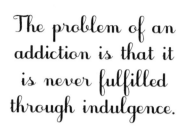

The problem of an addiction is that it is never fulfilled through indulgence.

As mothers, we have a lot at stake. The enemy will deceive you by tempting you to place your addiction above your children. Depending on what you crave, the enemy will design a script for you in which, moment by moment, day by day, you will miss out on fulfilling your calling as a mom. Before you know it, the season to sow into your children's lives will have passed you by. Don't hide in your room reading romance novels and eating ice cream bars while the television babysits your children. There is so much more to life.

As moms, a self-indulgent mindset deprives our children of their basic needs. Addictive behavior is often passed down from one generation to another. You likely have struggled with areas in which your mother or father struggled. If you do not find freedom in an area of addiction, the curse of your poor choices is often passed to your sons and daughters.

Addiction Destroys Families

Some of us have come into parenthood with a deficit. Our parents likely struggled with unresolved issues and unfulfilled needs. You and I did not have perfect parents, nor will we be perfect parents. Most children grow up with a "hole in their soul" that can only be met by the One and only perfect parent, Father God.

As we walk out the journey of parenthood, it is important we do not look to our own strength to walk in self-control. Our hope is to be so connected to Jesus that the life of His fruit-filled existence permeates our lives. If we are connected to His vine, we will bear the fruit of self-control.

Contentment Brings Clarity

Have you ever noticed that there is often truth on two separate sides of an issue? There is a paradoxical truth about the need for self-control, but there is an opposite side of the spectrum that we also need to talk about.

My friend, Teasi Cannon, wrote a book called *My Big Bottom Blessing*. In this book, she transparently talks about her life-long struggle with her body image. On the back of her book she comments, "Loving the girl in the mirror isn't about changing how you look but allowing God to change how you see." In one of her journal entries from June 28, 1997, she writes:

"I'm getting ready to go to sleep feeling overweight and defeated again.

I am full of the knowledge of how to get my weight off.

I know the key to my success is giving my pain to God instead of food…

Lord, Jesus, I need Your strength and mercy.

I need Your forgiveness, and most desperately

I need to see me as You see me…"

(Teasi Cannon, *My Big Bottom Blessing: How Hating My Body Led to Loving My Life*, Worthy Publishing, 2012, page 48).

Teasi continued on this roller coaster of trying to lose weight and failing. Her emotional pain led her to come to the bottom of herself and encounter God. She writes,

"If I had not been so utterly desperate to get answers about my big rear, I don't know that I would have ever found out what I really needed. I don't know that I would have seen how very little of God's love I was really experiencing or how selfish my love for others had been. Chances are, I would have been a wounded skinny chick, pretty on the outside but broken on the inside.

Ironically, whatever you despise most about yourself (it doesn't have to be weight) can become the catalyst for serious life change. Take that 'thing' and drop it down at the feet of Jesus. Then ask Him to help you get to the bottom of it. But be willing to *really* get to the bottom of it. The answer you get may not be the one you've wanted or expected, but it will be the one you *need*.

I'm still 'padded' today, but I love myself more than I ever have because I no longer let the devil define me." **(Teasi Cannon, *My Big Bottom Blessing: How Hating My Body Led to Loving My Life*, pages 201-202).**

> *Self-control is the fruit of the Spirit given to us by Jesus to walk closely with Him.*

Self-control is the fruit of the Spirit given to us by Jesus to walk closely with Him. Self-hatred is the fruit of the devil trying to use our human frailty against us.

This year I have read and embraced both Lysa's story in *Made to Crave* and Teasi's story in *My Big Bottom Blessing*. Both of these women have encountered God through their own struggles and pain.

As my thyroid and other health issues have impacted my weight gain and in some ways prevented my weight loss, I have needed to face my own roller coaster love affair with food.

Here is what is interesting. After going through a major health crises in my life, I am more thankful for my body than ever before. I look in the mirror and see a round, voluptuous figure that I love. I feel so content with who I am right now that I don't feel incredibly motivated to embrace the strenuous effort it will require for me to budge the scale. Both my nutritionist and nurse practitioner have encouraged me that as my body gets increasingly healthy, the weight will come off.

Healthy Self-Love

If we aren't careful, we remake God to suit our needs. In our quest to become Life-Giving Moms we need to both love God and ourselves. Jesus said,

> *"And you must love the Lord your God with all your heart, all your soul, all your mind, and all your strength. The second is equally important: 'Love your neighbor as yourself.' No other commandment is greater than these."*
> Mark 12:30-31, NLT

Jesus invites us on this intimate love journey where everything we are is required. He wants it all from us: heart, soul, mind, and strength. The good news is He gives it all back.

When we love Jesus first, we will love ourselves the most. We will not view God as a tyrant who demands our slavish obedience. We will see Him as the ruler of heaven and earth, but also as our friend.

Walking in the Fruit of the Holy Spirit Requires Walking with Jesus

Jesus encouraged those closest to Him that they could do nothing without Him (See John 15). Anything that you are trying to accomplish in your own strength will have no lasting value.

We tend to look at the outside while Jesus looks at the heart.

Exercising five hours a day in order to fit into skinny jeans is not necessarily the abundance that God promised us.

We tend to look at the outside while Jesus looks at the heart. You can be in the season of your greatest discipline with your physical body but be completely selfish with your time. The fruit that we find being connected to Jesus is not the fruit of being connected to the world. Holiness is not tied to a specific size and shape.

God calls us to a life of health. He wants us to be able to live long on this earth as we serve our families.

The Fruit of Self-Control is More Than What You Weigh

A few weightier questions of self-control are:
- Am I thinking pure and lovely thoughts about others?
- Am I forgiving others from the heart?
- Am I rejoicing when others rejoice?
- Am I jealous of the accomplishments of others?

Self-control involves so much more than what we put in our mouths. You cannot judge the fruit of self-control by what you see on the outside. God is the One who knows your thoughts and sees the attitudes of your heart. The way He judges is very different from the world.

Am I able, by the Spirit of God, to control the ugly self-life? God is not in heaven judging the size of your pants. We spend far too much time on earth thinking about how we look.

A Life-Giving Mom
Helps Her Children Live Healthy Lives

Healthy moms will help raise healthy children. Health begins from the inside out. Learning to forgive from the heart, speak with love, and rejoice with others are just a few of the healthy benefits of the fruit of self-control. The fruit of being connected to Jesus is that you will live a life of servanthood rather than selfishness. By His grace, you will be able to deny the self-indulgent excesses of the world and embrace the fidelity of loving Him first and others second. A Life-Giving Mom lives a life of health.

WATCH
Watch the free video
Replacing My Self-Indulgence with God's Self-Control
at www.SueDetweiler.com.

A PRAYER FOR
Self-Control

Jesus, You came to bring life and to bring it
more abundantly.
I am so sorry that at times I have wasted your
abundance on temporary things that will never satisfy.
You have made me to crave You.
As a mom, I can only give life to my kids
if I am connected to You, sustained by You.
Jesus, I admit my desperate and total need
for Your life-giving connection moment to moment.
I choose to deny myself my chosen
method of self-medicating.
I choose to closely walk with You,
being healed by our divine connection.
Jesus, you are the healer of my soul. I crave You.
I choose today to put You first in my life.
I choose to follow You daily
as I am a mother to my children.
I trust You to guide me. I trust You to counsel me.
I trust You to fill me with joy even when times are tough.
Jesus, I choose to embrace and embody
Your fruit of self-control.
Every time I choose to fill my deepest longings with
You, My children will see my total dependance on You.
I pray that my life example will inspire my children
to choose You.
You are my Life-Giver.
Your life breath already flows through my child.
May my child know you intimately in everyday life.

Love

Joy

Peace

Patience

Kindness

Goodness

Faithfulness

Gentleness

Self-Control

Chapter 11

LIFE-GIVING MOMS

GIVE LIFE

In my twenties, I was very judgmental of my parents, sharing my criticism of their relationship to my new husband in hopes we could have a life different than theirs.

Approaching her under the guise of religious zeal, I confronted my mother. In my youthful arrogance, I wanted her to take responsibility for the many mistakes and imperfections in our home. She said, "Sue, we did the best we could." At the time, I dismissed her response as a cop-out, too full of self-righteousness to see her wisdom in it all.

When it is time for a season to change, the imperfections of life are most visible. I have spent most of my life looking forward to the next season, sure that it will be better than the last. I am now at a season with four adult daughters and two sons not far behind. Looking back, I'm flooded with sweet memories of the time spent together making paper chains for birthdays and baking banana bread and my own peanut-butter popcorn, and family movie nights. Even the big work projects of cooking, painting, and planting flowers bring me joy. But it wasn't always like that. In the beginning, they wanted to help and were really just in the way. Then the season changed, and they were better than me at most things.

Soon my daughters will be mothers and my sons will be fathers. They will have so many choices in front of them bringing both excruciating pain and jubilation. No doubt, they will make mistakes, even some that we have made as parents. My prayer is that they will be life-giving parents.

On a walk with my mother this week, we talked about the changing season of my family. We sat down at a park bench next to some water. She looked at me, opened her hands and said, "When it is love, you let it go, and it comes back to you." The wisdom she has gained walking through life as my mom struck me.

When my daughters were ages 6, 4, 2, and newborn, I felt like I never had a break. I would need to get a babysitter just to go to the grocery store. I celebrated the freedom of walking the aisle pushing my cart. Later, at ages 2, 4, 6, and 8, we went everywhere together—packing our peanut butter sandwiches because we couldn't afford a drive-thru. Now we are more likely to go for a walk together or sit on the back porch with coffee. I am helping my daughter plan her wedding and paint her new home.

Learning to be a Life-Giving Mom without regrets requires embracing the season you are in. You have to let go of the past and live in the present as you lay hold of the future. At each transition you will likely shed some tears as you realize that you can't go back and re-

Learning to be a Life-Giving Mom without regrets requires embracing the season you are in.

live the past. You must move forward, facing the imperfections of your present, hoping for the future.

At the end of the Apostle Paul's life, he looked back as a father encouraging others to follow in his footsteps. He acknowledged the different seasons of life's race in this Scripture:

> *"I don't mean to say that I have already achieved these*
> *things or that I have already reached perfection.*
> *But I press on to possess that perfection for which*
> *Christ Jesus first possessed me.*
> *No, dear brothers and sisters, I have not achieved it,*
> *but I focus on this one thing:*
> *Forgetting the past and looking forward to what lies ahead,*
> *I press on to reach the end of the race and receive the heavenly*
> *prize for which God, through Christ Jesus, is calling us."*
> Philippians 3:12-14, NLT

Moms are not perfect—we are being perfected. Like Paul we are running this race in an imperfect world where stuff happens. Paul may not have had to deal with dirty diapers or teething babies, but he did have to be on the open seas after being shipwrecked. We all go through trials of life. It is in the trials that our character is being perfected.

We all need role models in different seasons, people we look to who bring encouragement for the journey. Every role model but One will fail. If we get up-close we will see that each one is imperfect, except the One Perfect Lamb who was crucified for our sins. He was the scapegoat. He was the rejected one.

Life-Giving Moms Let Go of the Past

If you have been a mom for a week you have probably already had some type of regret. After the fire when 6-week-old Rachel was in the hyperbolic chamber to bring more oxygen to her blood, I wept because I thought her life was already scarred by trauma. But it was only beginning. I have needed to watch all of my children struggle through things. Sometimes I was there to help wipe away the tears; sometimes I wasn't.

In addition to letting go of the hard times, you need to let go of the good times, too. Packing up the baby clothes and toys, or giving away the baby swing and then the swing-set… It becomes more difficult as time goes on. Rather than driving Barbie jeeps, your children will begin to drive their own cars and even have their own wrecks. Where did their tiny feet and hands go? Now I'm the one with the smallest feet in our family.

> *In addition to letting go of the hard times, you need to let go of the good times too.*

My daughter, Sarah, enjoyed sitting in her highchair more than any of our other children. Since she was our fourth, I had loosened up and just let her make a mess with her food. (I know you may be working on your child's manners and think, *Oh, how could you!*). Life is too short not to enjoy the messes that your children make. If Sarah Faith, who is now a 5'10" ravishing beauty, sat in the high-chair today and made a mess it would just be ridiculous. She is now a nanny to "her boys," and she also works at a nursing home and helps older people with their meals. The season is now passed, and the highchair is gone. I had to put these things away and keep the memories tucked safely away.

One of the hardest things about being a mom of six children, as well as a spiritual mom to others, is the finiteness of time. Whenever I pour my life into one of my children, I am not with another child. Most of my life as a mother I have felt pulled. As I lifted my own finiteness to God, He reminded me that one of the best gifts a mother can give a child is the gift of a sibling. The times that I haven't been at one of my child's events, chances are one of their siblings was there cheering them on.

Life-Giving Moms Don't Need to be Plagued by Mistakes

Take a moment right now and open up your hands to God. Close your eyes, and see Him putting your child in your hands. Now, lift your hands back to God. Give Him all of your children. You are simply a steward of His house. These are His children. He loves them more than you do. He has chosen to place these children in your arms for a short time. You have adopted these lonely ones into your home. They are not yours. They are His.

So knowing the briefness of your time with them, think about the common mistakes that moms regret:

- *not spending enough time*
- *missing events*
- *not being gentle or kind*
- *making a big deal over small things*
- *being too controlling*
- *not saying enough*
- *saying too much*
- *not being consistent in your own walk*
- *disciplining in anger*
- *not disciplining when you should*
- *being too rigid with boundaries*
- *not setting enough boundaries*
- *being distracted by things*
- *working too much*
- *talking too much*

- *not talking enough*
- *the need to listen more*
- *not condemning*
- *not judging*
- *giving clearer warnings*
- *giving more freedom for your child to make choices*
- *(list a few of your own regrets)*

Now think about the wisdom of my mother when she said, "We did the best we could." On a continuum of moms, 10 being *smug* (meaning you did most everything right) and 1 being *insecure* (meaning you did many things wrong), where would you place yourself?

<u>**10 (Smug)**</u>   <u>**1 (Insecure)**</u>

I did everything right.   *I did everything wrong.*

The problem with this continuum is that you are not a good judge. There are things you may think you did right that were really harmful for your child or things you think you did wrong that God used for your child's good.

A Life-Giving Mom puts her efforts as a mom in the hands of God. He is the only true judge. That means if you are hanging around judgmental mothers who are pointing fingers at you, you may need to set some boundaries. As imperfect as you are, God has entrusted you to be your children's mom—not *Pam Perfect.*

> A Life-Giving Mom puts her efforts as a mom in the hands of God.

and you cannot be fruitful unless you remain in me.
Yes, I am the vine; you are the branches.
Those who remain in me, and I in them, will produce much fruit.
For apart from me you can do nothing."
John 15:1-5, NLT

You become intimately connected with the Father through embracing Jesus as your Lord and Savior (See Romans 10:9-10). As you embrace His message, you are pruned and purified. As long as you stay connected to Him, you will bear fruit as a Life-Giving Mom. Apart from Him you can't do anything.

> *As you embrace His message, you are pruned and purified.*

A Life-Giving Mom is connected with the Eternal One who is able to see the past, present, and future at the same time. The key to your fruitfulness in the future is remaining in Christ. The good news is that you do not need to struggle and strain to bear fruit. You just stay connected to Him, walking with Him as your best friend. Jesus said these words to you:

"I have loved you even as the Father has loved me.
Remain in my love.
When you obey my commandments, you remain in my love,
just as I obey my Father's commandments and remain in his love.
I have told you these things so that you will be filled with my joy.
Yes, your joy will overflow!
This is my commandment:
Love each other in the same way I have loved you.
There is no greater love than to lay down one's life for

one's friends. You are my friends if you do what I command.
I no longer call you slaves, because a master doesn't confide
in his slaves. Now you are my friends, since I have told
you everything the Father told me.
You didn't choose me. I chose you.
I appointed you to go and produce lasting fruit, so
that the Father will give you whatever you ask for,
using my name. This is my command: Love each other."
John 15:9-17, NLT

You have been chosen by God to produce lasting fruit. The eternal fruit is your relationship with Him. The overflow of your intimate walk with Jesus as your best friend will be the opportunity for your children to find their life-source in and through Jesus.

As you walk with Jesus, resting your head on His heart, you will learn to know His Word, His will, and His ways. You will want to obey Him, not out of forced compliance, but out of heartfelt connection. Your joy will abound as you remain in His love.

You have been chosen by God to produce lasting fruit.

You are able to lay hold of your fruitful future by trusting, obeying, and loving your best friend. Even during the painful times when the past and present are being pruned from your life, it is with the promise of future fruitfulness. Your joy will be full even as tears steam down your cheeks.

You Can Do It

At the beginning of our journey together I shared the story about how I came alongside my daughter, Rachel, when she was running a race. I put my hand on her back and said, "You can do it!"

I hope that as you have read *9 Traits of a Life-Giving Mom* you have felt the hand of God Himself on your back running alongside you saying, "You can do it! You can be the best mom in the world for your child, with My help."

You are not alone. You are walking down this path of freedom with Jesus as your best friend. He will never leave you, nor forsake you. He won't forget you or get frustrated with you. He will never reject you or make you feel like you aren't good enough.

You can become all that God has created you to be. You will find healing and hope as you stay connected to your eternal life-source, Jesus. You can be assured that God will lead you through the imperfect places in your life.

Continue on your life-giving journey, letting go of those things that have held you back in the past. Travel forward with the expectancy that God is at work giving life. He prunes the hidden places of your heart. Go ahead and believe that He will continue to take your worst and replace it with His best.

Enjoy the journey. Dance along the path. Twirl with carefree abandonment. Remember, it is your role on earth to be a Life-Giving Mom. In heaven you will be a grace-filled daughter, giving all glory and honor to your life-giving Father.

A PRAYER TO BE A
Life-Giving Mom

JESUS,
YOU ARE THE SAME
YESTERDAY, TODAY, AND FOREVER.
YOU CONSISTENTLY LEAD ME INTO NEW SEASONS.
YOU HELP ME LET GO OF THE PAST,
LIVE IN THE PRESENT, AND LAY HOLD OF THE FUTURE.
I HAND OVER ALL OF MY MISTAKES AND REGRETS.
I KNOW THAT YOU WEAVE MY IMPERFECTIONS
INTO THE TAPESTRY OF MY LIFE.
YOU MAKE ALL THINGS BEAUTIFUL IN THEIR TIME.
I CHOOSE TO BE CONTENT.
I WILL CONSIDER ALL OF LIFE AS A GIFT FROM YOU.
I CHOOSE TO LIVE CAREFREE IN YOUR PRESENCE,
UNHURRIED, UNBURDENED, UNASHAMED.
I AM CASTING EVERY CARE I HAVE ONTO YOU.
I CAN DO NOTHING APART FROM YOU.
AS LONG AS I STAY CONNECTED TO YOU,
I WILL BEAR MUCH FRUIT.
JESUS, YOU ARE MY BEST FRIEND.
I LAY MY HEAD ON YOUR HEART.
I TRUST THAT WITH YOUR HELP
I WILL BE A LIFE-GIVING MOM

Study Guide

Study Guide
LESSON 1: LEARNING TO BE
A LIFE-GIVING MOM

All of life involves learning. We acquire skills as we practice. We also gain insight from others. The discovery process of becoming a Life-Giving Mom involves walking closely with God.

Every time I move into a new season with my children, I am entering into uncharted waters of the unknown. I often feel weak and in need of His grace.

> *"Each time he said, 'My grace is all you need.*
> *My power works best in weakness.'*
> *So now I am glad to boast about my weaknesses,*
> *so that the power of Christ can work through me."*
> 2 Corinthians 12:9, NLT

God has given you an amazing promise. His grace is sufficient for you as a mom. His power works best in our weakness. If you are feeling tired, stressed, or pulled in every direction, know that His power is working through your imperfections.

Join Nicole as she steps out of her kitchen and onto her front porch. If you have been a mom of small children, I am sure you can relate. Here's her story.

Nicole's Story
"The mental haze and physical exhaustion that come with young children had stripped away my normal nice-girl demeanor, and the

results weren't pretty. I wrestled with my out-of-control heart by taking it out on my husband, giving orders about the proper way to load the dishwasher, to bathe a child, to hold a pacifier, even the proper way to hug me ('Not a side hug, honey: I need a real *hug! Hug me like you mean it!')…*

I stepped out onto the front porch to throw my head back and roll my shoulders and try—again—to get my filter back in place, to get back to nice-girl-nice-mom-all-together status. With tears of frustration threatening to erupt like a thunderstorm, I looked down my pretty street: a predictable cul-de-sac, green lawns, blue skies, and pink crepe myrtles. My swirling thoughts defied my weariness, when that question raced in and parked itself in the front of my mind: Is being a Christian supposed to change me?

It was as if God sliced a cross-section of my spirit and laid it under a microscope. Every issue I struggled with in that afternoon—the internal twisting of my own heart…

Standing on my porch with a dish towel on one shoulder and burp cloth on the other, I knew in the deepest part of my soul that this could not be the 'life to the full' that Jesus promised." **(Nicole Unice, *She's Got Issues: Seriously Good News for Stressed-Out Secretly Scared Control Freaks Like Us*, Tyndale House Publishers, 2012, pages xii-xiii)**

Nicole's narrative beckons us as moms out of the mundane mom-stuff to expect Jesus to help us live life to the fullest at every stage of our lives.

You don't have to pretend to have everything all together. You can begin right where you are. What is the present struggle of your heart? Learn to let God into the middle of it.

> ❧ *You don't have to pretend to have everything all together.* ❧

Learning to be a Life-Giving Mom is to expect God in the ordinary moments of our lives. It is rocking your child to sleep, singing songs of praise as God's presence fills the room. It is staying connected to Jesus while changing diapers and cleaning up vomit.

Reflect on the following questions. I encourage you to pull out a prayer journal where you can more deeply write your reflections.

Reflection Questions

1. Nicole pondered this question: "Is being a Christian supposed to change me?" If so, what would living "life to the full" look like?

2. In the opening chapter, I describe what it was like to wake up with my house on fire. I was totally helpless. All I could do was drop to my knees and pray, "Help!" What situation in your life, as a mom, right now feels totally helpless?

3. After the fire, when we called my mom, we found out she had been praying for us. She prayed that we "would go through the fire and not be burned" (Isaiah 43). Have you prayed a life-saving prayer, or has someone prayed one for you?

4. Take a moment to reflect on the following statements from Chapter 1. Ask yourself, *Is this true of me?*
   • A Life-Giving Mom is connected to the ultimate Life-Giver.
   • A Life-Giving Mom overcomes tragedies.
   • A Life-Giving Mom is open to change.
   • A Life-Giving Mom is a life-long learner.

Group Discussion

What issue in your life feels overwhelming? How can we pray for you in your journey as a Life-Giving Mom?

Study Guide
LESSON 2: LEARNING TO REPLACE
MY ANGER WITH GOD'S LOVE

We have all messed up as moms. We have all blown it. Part of our growth and healing is admitting our mistakes and asking God to infuse us with His life to become a better mom. Ann Voskamp honestly talks about the daily struggle of replacing her anger with God's love.

Ann's Story

"I have been the mama who's punished when I needed to pray.
Who's hollered at kids when I needed to help *kids.*
Who's lunged forward—when I should have leaned on Jesus.
There are dishes stacked on the counter like memories and paint smeared on the table, and there are kids sprawled on the couch trying to read the same book at the same time—and there is only so much time.

I never expected love to be like this. I never expected so much joy. I never expected to get so much wrong...

And no matter how the craziness of this whole parenting thing all turns out: The reward of loving is in the loving; loving is itself the great outcome of loving. The success of loving is in how we change *because we kept on loving—regardless of any thing else changing...*

That godly parenting isn't ultimately about rules—*but having a* relationship *with an ultimate God and His children.*

That godly parenting isn't fueled by my efforts—but by God's grace.

That if I make God first and am most *satisfied in His love—then I'm released to love my children fully and satisfactorily.*

That maybe it all comes down to this:
My kids don't need to see a Super Mama.
They need to see a Mama who needs a Super God."
(Ann Voskamp, "Why Your Kids Don't Need a Super Mama"
Blog on AHolyExperience.com, July 16, 2013.)

I agree with Ann. Our children do not need a "Super Mama." They need a "Super God." The beauty of being a family is that we are all a part of God's redemptive masterpiece. God has made you, and each of your children, to be His work of art. He even brings the broken pieces of our lives to form a beautiful mosaic of His love.

"For we are God's masterpiece.
He has created us anew in Christ Jesus, so we can
do the good things he planned for us long ago."
Ephesians 2:10, NLT

You have been created and intended for good works that God Himself prepared for you. When you have an angry outburst with your children, God does not disqualify you from being their mom. The enemy wants hostility to be in your home. God restores your home with His love and forgiveness. He repairs broken relationships with the power of His presence and healing in your lives.

Reflection Questions

1.   How was anger expressed in your home when you were growing up? Was there someone who tended to be an "exploder"? Was there a member of your family who gave the "silent treatment"? How did you deal with your anger in your family of origin?

2. I shared openly about my own struggle with my negative thought patterns that led to angry outbursts. The enemy often puts thoughts in our mind that lead us toward conflict and resentment. Because Jesus has given us the "mind of Christ," we are able to replace ungodly thoughts and beliefs with statements of truth. Here is an example of replacing an ungodly thought with a godly thought:

Ungodly Thought	Godly Thought
I'm the worst mom in the world	I am becoming a better mom
I always blow it	I can do all things through Christ
I can't help it	I can choose to love
God, can you hear me?	God hears my cry

What are your ungodly thoughts? Name a godly thought.

3. Without faith it is impossible to please God (Hebrews 11:6). Write down specific declarations about your calling as a mom. After writing each statement down, read them out loud in faith.
   - I will walk in love as a mom.
   - I am forgiven for my past sins.
   - I am free from resentment and bitterness.
   - I can enjoy my children and not be irritated or annoyed.

Group Discussion

How do you personally deal with anger? Do you tend to hold your anger in and deal with resentment? Do you let your anger out and struggle with outbursts? How has this impacted your relationships in your home?

How can we pray for you?

Study Guide
LESSON 3: LEARNING TO REPLACE
MY SADNESS WITH GOD'S JOY

I remember spending a day in bed as a young mother, curled in a fetal position with feelings of sadness washing over me. Finally, I got out of bed the next morning to take a prayer walk. I had given birth to my third baby just six weeks before, and my hormones were making havoc on my emotions.

As I walked, I looked up and saw a brilliant sunrise. The glorious golden colors brightened my mood. God wove into the fabric of creation His love song of redemption. No matter how tough the day before, the sunrise is a mark of the arrival of a new day. I could face the demands of motherhood again because I knew deep in my heart that God is good.

For many of us, being a mom is much harder than what we thought. Sarah Mae expresses how parenting did not come easily or naturally for her.

Sarah Mae's Story

"Getting awakened multiple times a night, every night, is enough to make anyone crash, but add the weight of having to function through the day in order to take care of a one-, two-, and four-year-old, and this mama was spent before the day began. Just knowing the strength and energy that would be required to make it through the day was enough to sway me to stay balled up under warm covers. Serious sleep deprivation combined with the constant giving of myself, soothing cries, breaking up fights, training, disciplining, and trying to stay calm and gentle in

the middle of it all was breaking me. I needed help. I so badly needed someone to call who could come and rescue me, just for one day. But that wasn't my reality…

Down to the bone, to the deepest part of my soul, is the love I have for my children. Every day of my life is imperfectly offered to them. But the little years, they're hard and oftentimes lonely. It's like a secret we fear sharing, just how life-altering motherhood is, especially when you don't have training or support. Let me pull back the curtain on the idea that just because you love and are thankful to be a mother, parenting will come easily or naturally. The lifetime commitment that is motherhood will, many days, stretch you beyond what you think you can handle."
(Sarah Mae Hoover and Sally Clarkson, *Desperate: Hope for the Mom Who Needs to Breathe,* **Thomas Nelson, 2013, pages xv-xvii.)**

Each of us is born with a child-like hope and expectancy of a bright future. When we get covered up with the mundane responsibilities of feeding babies, changing diapers, and doing housework, we can fail to experience the wonder of God's love.

You might be functioning at a deficit in mothering. Maybe you didn't have a good role model or a mom who consistently walked in joy. Your mom's unresolved emotions negatively impacted your childhood.

Stormie Omartian experienced the emotional torment and instability of her mother's emotions. Her mother locked Stormie in a closet when she was a child to discipline her. The scarring on her own life needed the healing touch of Jesus.

Stormie's Story

"I tried everything I knew to get out of that [emotional] closet of pain. I drank impressive quantities of alcohol, took dangerous amounts of drugs, went deeply into eastern religions, the occult, and unhealthy

relationships. But these things gave me nothing more than a temporary relief, after which I was worse off than before. I became more and more depressed, fearful, anxious, and hopeless, until finally I couldn't stand the pain any longer. I wanted to die...

When I met Pastor Jack [Hayford], he talked to me about Jesus in a way that made Him sound amazingly real and very much like a close and loving friend. He helped me understand that most of my problems existed because I was separated from God and the only way to bridge that separation was to receive Jesus as my Savior...

Right after I received Jesus as my Savior that day in Pastor Jack's office, I noticed a difference in my life. I had a feeling of peace, of being accepted, of being cleansed from all my past failure, of starting over with a clean slate. And I felt love, joy, and hope for the first time. I also had a growing sense of purpose, and I began to see a future for my life."
(Stormie Omartian, "Stormie's Story," StormieOmartian.com)

Maybe you have been locked into an emotional closet just like Stormie was. You need Jesus and the help of others to get you unlocked from the past. In God's presence is the fullness of joy.

Reflection Questions

1. Sarah Mae reflects on how motherhood is tougher than she anticipated. Are parts of motherhood more difficult than you expected?

2. In chapter 3, I shared about the downward staircase of "stinkin' thinkin'," which leads to a dark place emotionally. Do you have any patterns of negative thoughts that put you in an emotional closet?

3. We are challenged in 2 Corinthians 10:3-5 to "take captive every thought to make it obedient to Christ." For stubborn recurring thoughts it can be helpful to have a "replacement" thought.

Reflect on these examples:

Ungodly Thought	Godly Thought
My life never gets better	Tomorrow is a new day
I have nothing to live for	I live for Christ
I can't do anything	I can do all things through Christ

Joy is a fountain that flows from God's presence. Stormie talked about the emotional closet that she dealt with after being locked in a physical closet by her mother. What things from your "emotional closet" do you need to clear out to make more room for joy in your life?

Group Discussion

What specific situations in your life as a mom trigger your own negative thoughts and emotions?

How can we pray for you?

Study Guide

LESSON 4: LEARNING TO REPLACE MY ANXIETY WITH GOD'S PEACE

Learning to replace my anxiety with God's peace requires me, as a mom, to learn how to really pray. Moms are known to worry. We can be nervous for our children's first day of kindergarten or when they are first learning to ride a bike or learning to drive a car. No matter their age, we are tempted to worry.

If we aren't careful, our times of prayer will deteriorate to little more than a mental rehearsal of all the things we are anxious about. The good news is that Jesus is the Prince of Peace—your peace. When we come to Him daily, we can exchange our anxiety for His peace. Our character is being developed as we learn to walk with God intimately. Like any relationship, it takes time and effort to know God's heart and ways.

The hard part about going deeper in our prayer life as a mom is that we are on call 24/7. The good news is, as you learn to pray, you are also teaching your children about God.

When Rachel was 3, I was reading my Bible in bed. She nestled close to me as we read Psalm 23 together:

> *"The Lord is my shepherd;*
> *I have all that I need.*
> *He lets me rest in green meadows;*
> *He leads me beside peaceful streams.*
> *He renews my strength.*
> *He guides me along right paths, bringing honor to his name.*

Even when I walk through the darkest valley,
I will not be afraid, for you are close beside me.
Your rod and your staff protect and comfort me."
Psalm 23:1-4, NLT

The name "Rachel" means little lamb. So as we read about God being our shepherd who leads and guides us, we realized that this was "Rachel's Psalm." We wrote this on top of the chapter in my Bible. When Rachel turned 16, I gave her my Bible with all my notes. She still calls Psalm 23 her Psalm.

With more children, I grew desperate for God's peace. I began to build strategies into my life so that I would cultivate peace in my heart before the demands of the day began. The Bible became my lifeline. Gone were the moments of having uninterrupted time whenever I wanted to spend time with God. Now I had to strategize, fight for, and improvise to have that time.

I kept my Bible handy with a bookmark in it, ready to read when I nursed the baby. It wasn't uncommon to find my Bible on the bathroom floor. I would flip my head over to blow-dry my hair and read the Word. I began to take prayer walks with the double-wide stroller. I would pray out loud with a prayer list in my hands. With worship music up high in the house, I took dance breaks with my children in my arms—my dance of survival when the days grew rough.

Building daily structures into my life and our home became pleasant boundaries of health, and freedom from anxiety. The most important boundary for me was setting aside a time when I was alone with God. One morning Angela woke up and was pulling on my arm. "Mommy, I want breakfast."

"Mommy has to eat first. Then I will get you breakfast." Angela looked puzzled and began to look around for the hidden food that I might be eating. All she could see was my Bible on my lap.

"Do you eat the Bible for breakfast, Mama?" I laughed and kissed her. "That's right, sweetie. Mommy has to eat the Bible first. Then I can make you breakfast." That gave me 10 more minutes.

You are developing your own spiritual history with God and your children. The beauty and depth of the seeds you have sown will only be seen in eternity. Every day you have the opportunity to build healthy habits that develop God's peace.

Our anxiety is not limited to what could happen to our children. You may have experienced the loss of a job, or a health issue. It's important in those times that you learn to pour out your heart to God in prayer.

I really respect Kay Arthur's daily walk with God. She shares a difficult moment in her life journey where she found God's peace through prayer.

Kay's Story

"I WAS A FAILURE. I was convinced of it. I had failed God, and there was nothing I could do about it. I was impotent to change my circumstances. Disappointment overwhelmed me. My dreams for being a missionary had been shattered...

Little did I know that the onset of chest pains would keep my dreams from coming true. The chest pains began without warning and kept getting worse. Often I found myself nearly out of breath. Jack insisted I see a doctor. The examination and cardiogram revealed that I had pericarditis, an infection in the lining of my heart. I was confined to bed...

Through my physical weakness I had brought Jack's thirteen-year missionary career to a halt... Before becoming a missionary Jack had sold insurance, but that had been so long ago, and I wanted a husband in some sort of full-time ministry...

For weeks I lived in torment of mind and heart, until the morning I rolled out of bed onto my knees and prayed, 'Father, whatever You want.

If You want Jack to sell insurance again, it's okay; I will accept it.' God could do as He pleased. He was the Potter—I the clay. That morning on my knees I surrendered my expectations, my desires, and my evaluations to my God. And in my submission came my PEACE." **(Kay Arthur, As Silver Refined: Answers to Life's Disappointments, Waterbrook Press, 2011, pages 9-11)**

Like Kay, you will have many opportunities to roll out of bed and onto your knees to pray. The torment in your mind and heart will cease when you surrender your anxious thoughts to God. His peace is available to all who seek Him.

Reflection Questions

1. Look again at these *9 Healthy Habits that Bring God's Peace.* Check those habits that are already a part of your life. Circle the specific habits that you believe God is calling you to concentrate on right now.

Healthy Habits that Bring God's Peace

- Reading the Bible (Replacing the world's words with God's Word.)
- Prayer & Meditation (Replacing my concerns with God's care.)
- Forgiveness (Replacing my hurt with God's health.)
- Journaling (Reframing tough situations with God's strategy.)
- Church Community (Replacing my apathy with God's passion.)
- Books (Replacing my confusion with God's clarity.)
- Podcasts (Restoring my foggy brain with God's focus.)
- Conferences (Reshaping my weakness with God's power.)
- Counseling (Rebuilding my brokenness with God's wholeness.)

2. Meditate on the promise of peace in Isaiah, which is a song of praise sung to God:

"You will keep in perfect peace all who trust in you,
all whose thoughts are fixed on you!"
Isaiah 26:3, NLT

3. In your prayer journal, write down your personal commitment to God to trust Him and fix your thoughts on His peace.

Group Discussion

What healthy habits from the list above is God calling you to concentrate on? How does your life of prayer impact your role as a mom?

How can we pray for you?

Study Guide
LESSON 5: LEARNING TO REPLACE
MY FRUSTRATION WITH GOD'S PATIENCE

As a young mom I found that whenever I tried to escape from my children, they would only want me more. In my mind I was just trying to get "me time" to take a bath or read a book. It always backfired.

Whenever our focus is on ourselves, we will succumb to the strain of the day. When we start blaming our children for how we are feeling, we will lose patience with their needs and blunders.

Lisa Bevere reflects on how God used the struggle of being a mom to show her own brokenness.

Lisa's Story

"I found myself under intense pressure such as I had never experienced before. My second son had recently been born. My oldest son was two years old and suddenly very uncooperative about going down for afternoon naps…

One day during just such a struggle, I snapped. I grabbed my two-year-old and stormed upstairs. I thought to myself, I must make him see that he is not to get off his bed again… *He struggled, kicked, and squirmed. I thought,* I need to slam this child against the wall… *I raised him eye level and was just about to shove him when I saw the fear in his eyes…*

At that moment I realized the problem did not lie with my parents, my husband, my children, [my] pressures, my upbringing, my ethnic background, or my hormones—it was with me…

For the first time I felt the entire ugly weight of it on my shoulders. It was as if all the scenes of hateful words and actions were replayed to me, scenes in which I thought I had been justified. Now as I watched them replay in my mind I was horrified by my reactions...

Broken, I cried for help, 'God, I don't want this anymore. I will no longer justify it or blame it on anyone else. Forgive me, Lord.' In that moment I felt Him lift the weight of sin and guilt from me. I cried all over again, but this time it was with relief." **(Lisa Bevere, *Out of Control and Loving it!* Creation House, 1996, pages 123-124.)**

Lisa found that when she was blaming everyone and everything else it was really her own problem. If you are finding yourself constantly frustrated over recurring issues, it's time to reevaluate. What is the root of your frustration?

A major breakthrough happened for me when I stopped seeing my children as an interruption. As a working mom, many of my work hours were at home. With the pressure of deadlines, I can get so focused on what I need to do that I forget the reason I am staying at home. I am here for my children. They are my priority.

Jesus said to His disciples:

"'So you want first place? Then take the last place. Be the servant of all.'
He put a child in the middle of the room. Then, cradling the
little one in his arms, he said, 'Whoever embraces one of
these children as I do embraces me, and far
more than me—God who sent me.'"
Mark 9:35-37, MSG

We are serving God when we serve our children. Our role as mom is to be servant of the whole household. I will have patience as I begin each day ready to serve rather than be served. When I "die" to my own selfish agenda, I gain fresh life from God. When I put my children's needs above my own, I am embracing God's call on my life.

When I set out to serve my children first, I don't lose my patience. When I serve my children first, they become less clingy as I meet their needs. When I serve my children first, life is more fun.

Reflection Questions

1. Meditate on 1 Peter 5:5-6 in *The Amplified Bible*. Write down specific ways that you need to clothe yourself with humility as a mom.

2. The character trait of patience is developed through an intimate walk with God. I gave some examples of how, as a new mom, I began to spend time with God. Take time now to list some of your strategies for your present season of walking with God.

3. Hurt moms hurt their children. Reflect on times you have recently become frustrated with your children. Write down specific things that may have triggered your impatience. Now, ask God to show you ways to defuse your frustration.

Group Discussion

Share a time when you lost patience with your children. (Remember: There are no perfect parents, only a perfect God. There are also no perfect children.)

Do you tend to blame your children for your frustration? What daily strategies help you walk in patience? How can the group come alongside you?

Study Guide
LESSON 6: LEARNING TO REPLACE
MY NEGATIVITY WITH GOD'S KINDNESS

As you and I walk with God, He seems to sneak up on us with His kind of surprises. He is the master designer of our lives. We may react negatively to His blessed interruptions called children, but His plan always brings life.

Mary, the mother of Jesus, had every reason to reject God's plan. When told that she would conceive God's child, even though she was a young virgin, Mary responded, "I am the Lord's servant. May everything you have said about me come true." (Luke 1:38, NLT)

Part of being a Life-Giving Mom is being willing to embrace God's plan for our lives. His plan will always demonstrate a supernatural loving kindness that is beyond human comprehension.

Priscilla Shirer was also surprised. She needed to surrender her own agenda and embrace what God was doing. Here is her story.

Priscilla's Story

"After three years of marriage, with little effort, God allowed me to get pregnant. We were thrilled. Soon, however, almost before the reality of 'baby makes three' had even begun to hit us, I miscarried...

Life. Interrupted again.

How could this happen? Why would God allow it? Did it mean we'd never be able to have children? Could we possibly get past this horrible experience and dare to try again, knowing how low the lows can be when your joy is snatched away?

Yes, we could.

Yes, we did.

First came Jackson. Then two years later, Jerry Jr. And when these fun little guys began rounding the corner from toddlerhood to the school-age years, Jerry and I decided we were closing up shop in the baby-making business. We both loved being parents but were so looking forward to life without diapers, sippy cups and colicky crying spells in the middle of the night...

When those faint pink lines shaded their way into a plus-sign on the pregnancy test... Jerry's and my plan for a new phase of life suddenly became our plan for an unexpected phase of life....

One day in the midst of my self-imposed pity party, I got the feeling God was asking me a question... Was I going to surrender myself completely to Him? Was I going to embrace His plans for me?

Turns out God was about to send me another *blessed interruption.*

Not just Jude, my new little son, but Jonah." **(Priscilla Shirer,** ***Life Interrupted: Navigating the Unexpected.*** **B & H Publishing Group, 2011, pages 3-8.)**

Like Mary and Priscilla, we need to surrender our preferences and surrender to God's will. As you and I yield ourselves completely to God, we will live out His call. Embracing the surprises of our lives helps us to live with a good attitude.

Knowing that life is a gift from God will guard against our own sense of entitlement as parents. If you and I feel entitled to our own free time or expendable income we will be disappointed.

Children will spend our extra income and they will require more time than we could fathom. If we view our children like an inconvenience, we will treat them like one.

The fruit of God's kindness is a remarkable force of persuasion in the lives of our children. Being friendly to their friends and generous with our time will plant good seeds in their hearts. Being warmhearted, affectionate, caring, and considerate will overwhelm the enemy as we embrace God's plan of serving our children sacrificially. His loving kindness will cover sins and heal wounds.

Reflection Questions

1. We all have negative patterns and cycles we go through in relationships with our family. It is part of being an imperfect parent. As you read through the chapter and I shared some of my negative patterns, what patterns in your life are areas where you feel you need God's help for you to show more kindness to your children?

2. I began an experiment to very consciously speak positive affirmations over my sons who heard negative statements all their lives. The power of being positive helps build more positive connections. Are there any strategies God is showing you to help your children experience God's kindness through you?

3. I made up a title for a book called *Negative Parenting Tips: How to Wound Your Child Through Neglect, Emotional Instability, Harsh Correction, and Over-Permissiveness.* In what ways do you struggle with the four parenting traps that I listed? Reflect and list the positive characteristic you would like to have as a parent.

Negative Parenting Trap	Godly Parenting
• Neglect	
• Emotional Instability	
• Harsh Correction	
• Over-Permissiveness	

Group Discussion

How does parenting trigger your own sense of entitlement? Do you feel like you have a right to your free time and expendable income? How do the interruptions of life affect your behavior toward your children? What negative parenting pattern would you like to overcome?

Study Guide

LESSON 7: LEARNING TO REPLACE MY MANIPULATION WITH GOD'S GOODNESS

Christian parents can get trapped in the pattern of trying to control their child's behavior. Most of the time the motive is that we truly want the best for our children. However, we can have other religious motives, like desiring to look good in the eyes of others.

Lisa Harper's story of a mischievous kindergartner illustrates how often religious parents are concerned about their own reputations.

Lisa's Story

"Instead of sweetly singing a Bible camp song, her mischievous kindergartner had cleared his throat and burst forth in a ribald tune about cigarettes and beer! Teresa and I got so tickled that morning talking about all the ways children embarrass and disappoint their parents, especially in 'religious' settings! Because even mild-mannered children don't always behave appropriately in church or in front of our 'church friends.' And some parents get really bent out of shape about it—as if their spiritual reputation is somehow dependent upon what pops out of their offsprings' mouths or how much the kids fidget in the pew on Sunday.

Our conversation reminded me of how very different our heavenly Father's character is. Every single one of His children has rebelled in some way or another. We've thrown temper tantrums, shoving our fists in His holy face and arrogantly demanding that the King of Kings give us different circumstances. We often misbehave like strong-willed kindergartners, too, determined to do whatever we want." (**Lisa Harper, Relentless Love: God's Faithfulness in the Face of Human Failure, Howard Publishing Comany, Inc., 2002, page 2.**)

If you are overly concerned with your reputation as a parent, you will be sorely disappointed by the behavior of your children. Just like you are an imperfect parent, they are imperfect children. You can't manipulate them to do what you want.

Guiding our children in God's ways still requires their choice of whether they will receive Jesus as their Savior. As they grow older, they will have many choices on a daily basis. Part of their learning process will involve failing. We have the opportunity to be a bridge to God. It is God's goodness that leads our children to repentance.

When children grow into their own adult relationship with Jesus, they are able to hear God's voice. They are able to be led and guided by Him. From the least to the greatest, our children are able to learn to walk in God's ways.

Sometimes it is after our children have made poor choices that they turn toward God. If you manipulate or control them, it often just drives them into rebellion. They need to choose God from their own hearts.

A Life-Giving Mom trusts God with the fate of her children. You have a responsibility to instruct, warn, guide, and challenge, but also to love and forgive your children. When you truly put your children in God's hands, you are able to see Him transform their hearts from the inside out.

Reflection Questions

1. In chapter 7, I shared how difficult it is to deal with a rebellious son or daughter. I recommend that you consider this plan of action:
   - Humble yourself.
   - Seek Godly counsel and partnership.
   - Become a learner and gain new parenting skills.
   - Admit your imperfections and mistakes.

- Be firm, steadfast, and consistent.
- Put your trust in the goodness of God.
- Gain new confidence that with God's help you can be the best mom for your child.

What part of this plan do you need to put into action?

2. How do you react when your children misbehave? Are you embarrassed? Are you defensive? Have you made any poor parenting choices because you were concerned about your reputation?

3. In your journal, write a letter to your child. It may just be a private letter where you express your feelings but you don't share with anyone. It may be a letter of repentance like I wrote. Ask the Holy Spirit to help you embody God's goodness that leads a child to repentance.

Group Discussion

How did your parents discipline you for rebellion? Describe a situation when you fell into a parenting trap and tried to manipulate or control your children. How did it go?

How can we pray for you?

Study Guide
LESSON 8: LEARNING TO REPLACE
MY FEAR WITH GOD'S FAITHFULNESS

What happens when you are suddenly faced with your worst fears? As parents, we fear for the safety of our children. If you allow fear to take control, you will likely fall into fear-based parenting.

Linda Barrick awoke to her worst nightmare when her whole family was in a car accident.

Linda's Story

"I opened my eyes. My face was smashed against a windshield of crushed glass. How did I get here? Is this a dream? Wasn't I just sitting with my husband and son watching our fifteen-year-old, Jen, sing in the choir at her school's fall concert?

I reached down with my right hand to touch my leg, and when I lifted my hand up again it was covered with blood. This can't be real. Lord, please wake me up!

'Mom? Mom!' I heard Josh calling for me from the backseat. I couldn't turn around to see him, but I answered anyway.

'Josh! Josh!'

'Mom!'

'Is this real?!' I asked. 'Is it a dream?' I didn't hear an answer so I said again, 'Is this real?'

'Yes, Mom, this is real.'

In anguish, I cried out, 'Lord Jesus, please help us! Come to our rescue! Save us!'

As a mom, I wanted with every molecule inside me to hug Josh and touch him and make him feel better. I wanted to hold Jen in my arms and tell her that I loved her. But I couldn't move. The crushed metal and broken glass encased my body like a giant, sinister glove. The only thing I could do was pray." **(Linda Barrick, *Miracle for Jen: A Tragic Accident, Mother's Desperate Prayer, and Heaven's Extraordinary Answer*, Tyndale House Publishers, Inc., 2012, pages 1-2)**

> *Train your mind and heart to anchor on God's character found in His Word.*

This was just the beginning of Linda's journey with her daughter, Jen, as she recovered from life-threatening injuries. She needed to trust in the faithfulness of God.

Jesus often comforted His disciples in their fear. He did heroic feats where He walked on the water and told them to not be afraid (John 6:15-21). Jesus was fearless in the face of His own death and predicted that it was coming (John 8:21-28). Jesus did not allow fear to control Him or stop Him from following the Father's will. Jesus modeled a fearless faith.

Fear inhibits your ability to be a Life-Giving Mom. Fear manifests itself in dread, anxiety, panic, agitation, distress, unease, and many other forms. It hinders your ability to think clearly and blocks the flow of the Holy Spirit in your life.

Train your mind and heart to anchor on God's character found in His Word. If you have God's Word memorized and hidden in your heart, then when you are facing a tragedy, His perspective floods your mind.

God's faithfulness is seen in how He helps us with the little and big things in our lives. Carol Cymbala tells about how she has experienced God's faithfulness.

Carol's Story

"There are so many things in this life we don't understand. But God is sovereign; he's God. He has everything under control, and he knows what's best.

Listen, I've prayed about overcoming my shyness and my feelings of inadequacy. God's helped me overcome my inadequacies, but I'm still shy. I still get nervous when I have to speak in front of people. But he gives me the strength to handle it. God does for me what he did for the apostle Paul, who prayed for God to remove the thorn, but instead God said, 'My power is made perfect in weakness' (2 Corinthians 12:9).

'Sometimes a situation may not turn out the way we want, but if we put it in God's hands, then no matter how it comes out, it will be right—even though we might endure pain. That's why we have to trust him totally. God can absolutely be depended on." **(Carol Cymbala, "Finding God Faithful," TodaysChristianWoman.com)**

We need to totally trust God and learn to lean on His faithfulness. *His faithfulness will drive out every form of fear. Your emotions will be steadied by His consistency in your life.*

Reflection Questions

1. Look at the variety of words that describe types of fear that you may experience in your life. Circle all the words that apply. Underline the top three.

dread	anxiety	panic	agitation	fright
distress	worry	alarm	angst	unease
creeps	shivers	terror	nerves	horror
phobia	nightmare	scared	foreboding	danger
apprehension	nervous	jumpy	insecurity	jitters

2. Write down the main situations in your life that have prompted you to feel fearful.

3. Write a personal prayer of entrusting God with each situation. Use Scriptures that teach about God's faithfulness.

Group Discussion

What type of situation triggers fear in your life? Share a time when you pressed through your fear and found God to be faithful.

How can we pray for you?

Study Guide
LESSON 9: LEARNING TO REPLACE MY PRIDE WITH GOD'S GENTLENESS

Pride hides under a religious robe. The danger of pride is that you usually don't know that you are trapped by it. Pride responds to your children in harsh tones. Pride creates a distance between you and others.

Joyce Meyer talks about pride.

Joyce's Story

"There is a deceptive sin that can keep us from walking in love: pride. It's deceptive because when you have pride, you're usually too proud to admit it. I know this because I used to have teachings on pride and they didn't sell well...

Pride is an independent, me-oriented spirit. It makes people arrogant, rude and hard to get along with. When our heart is prideful, we don't give God the credit and we mistreat people, looking down on them and thinking we deserve what we have...

I realize this is a hard message to hear. But we need to be honest about pride in our lives because if we aren't, we will create a separation between us and God. And that's the worst condition we can be in. If you want to check your heart to see if you're proud in an ungodly way, ask yourself:

- *How am I treating people?*
- *How do I think about others?*
- *Do I talk about myself more than I talk about God and what He's done?*

The good news is, we can humble ourselves and turn a bad situation around. Give God the glory for the good things in your life, and show His righteousness by helping others—the poor, needy and oppressed. Make it all about Jesus." (**Joyce Meyer, "Do You Need to Get Over Yourself?" https://www.joycemeyer.org/articles/ea.aspx?article=get_over_yourself, accessed December 13, 2013.**)

Pride was the garment the Pharisees wore as they enforced harsh rules on the people. Jesus was amazingly merciful with the woman caught in adultery, and with Zacchaeus, the tax collector. It was the Pharisees, Sadducees, and Scribes whom Jesus rebuked for their pride. They were the ones who were trying to follow God's rules and live righteously. The only problem was they couldn't see their sin of pride.

1 Peter 5:5 in *The Amplified Bible* sheds light on how to overcome the pride in our lives:

> *"...Clothe (apron) yourselves, all of you, with humility*
> *[as the garb of a servant, {so that its covering cannot possibly*
> *be stripped from you, with freedom from pride and arrogance]*
> *toward one another. For God sets Himself against the proud*
> *(the insolent, the overbearing, the disdainful, the presumptuous,*
> *the boastful)—[and He opposes, frustrates, and defeats them],*
> *but gives grace (favor, blessing) to the humble.*
> 1 Peter 5:5 AMP

Our job as moms is to get dressed every day like a servant. The clothing of humility needs to be a part of how we relate to our children. When we walk in pride, it is God Himself who opposes our overbearing manner with our children. He gives grace, favor, and blessing to us when we are humble.

Being a mom is a position of leadership in the home. Like any role of leadership, we can abuse it when we walk in pride. Our children already see our mistakes. It's far better for us to humbly admit our weakness and receive God's help to overcome it.

When we walk in gentleness with our children, we are being careful to care for them as God treats us. Every child needs to be disciplined, challenged, instructed, and warned. But let's remember that Jesus already took their punishment for them when He died on the cross for their sins. Each child is different in how they need to be treated.

Gentleness is often an overlooked fruit of the Holy Spirit that prevents you from injuring the heart of your child. When you express the gentle heart of Jesus, you give your children an opportunity for a "do-over." You allow them to know how to make mistakes and then get back on the right track.

It's important to point out that gentleness is not the same thing as passivity. Passivity just hides behind its responsibility to discipline your child. Passivity looks for the path of least resistance. Passivity allows the situation to get out of hand. Passivity breeds rebellion.

Gentleness is a bridge of reconciliation to the Father in heaven. Gentleness is the loving hand of a mom who wipes away the tears of a child who failed, but wants to do better.

Walking in humility and gentleness is key to your child feeling safe with you. They are more likely to open up and share their heart if they know they will receive a gentle response from you.

Reflection Questions

1. In Chapter 9, I described the destructiveness of pride. Look back and write down some quotes you feel are fitting about pride.

2. Reread the story of the woman with the alabaster flask in Luke
    7:37-50. Can you think of three things you learn from the way
    Jesus relates to her? Are there situations in your relationship with
    your children where you can apply the gentleness of Christ?

3. Does Joyce Meyer's description of pride help you look at your
    own need to walk in God's gentleness?

4. As a parent, there may be times when you make a mistake of
    judgment. Are you able to admit your mistakes to your children?
    Are you able to admit to others in your household when you
    have walked in pride?

Group Discussion

Every family is different, with different age combinations. What
do you see as the difference between gentleness and passivity in your
relationship with your child at this stage?

Discuss ways each of you can walk in a greater quality of God's
gentleness this week.

How can we pray for you?

Study Guide
LESSON 10: LEARNING TO REPLACE MY SELF-INDULGENCE WITH GOD'S SELF-CONTROL

Ask yourself, "When I am stressed, what do I turn to?" Do you find yourself thinking about your problems as you search the pantry for something to eat? Or do you escape from your problems by reading a romance novel or shopping? Anything that you use to satisfy your deepest longings outside of God will never answer the desires of your soul.

We have been made to crave God. The only thing that truly satisfies us is a vital relationship with Him. He calls us to follow Him. He wants to be the leader in our relationship. Jesus said,

> *"Anyone who intends to come with me has to let me lead.*
> *You're not in the driver's seat; I am. Don't run from suffering;*
> *embrace it. Follow me and I'll show you how.*
> *Self-help is no help at all.*
> *Self-sacrifice is the way, my way, to saving yourself,*
> *your true self. What good would it do to get everything*
> *you want and lose you, the real you?*
> *What could you ever trade your soul for?"*
> Mark 8:34-37, MSG

To follow after Jesus we need to dethrone our self-centeredness and truly follow Him. Lysa TerKeurst, author of *Made to Crave*, says it like this:

Lysa's Story

"When Jesus says, 'Follow me,' it's not an invitation to drag our divided heart alongside us as we attempt to follow hard after God. When Jesus wants us to follow Him—really follow Him—it's serious business. Here's how Jesus describes it:

> *'If anyone would come after me, he must deny*
> *himself and take up his cross and follow me.'*
> Mark 8:34 ESV

With Jesus, if we want to gain, we must give up.

If we want to be filled, we must deny ourselves.

If we want to truly get close to God, we'll have to distance ourselves from other things.

If we want to conquer our cravings, we'll have to redirect them to God.

God made us capable of craving so we'd have an unquenchable desire for more of Him, and Him alone. Nothing changes until we make the choice to redirect our misguided cravings to the only one capable of satisfying them.

Getting healthy is not just about losing weight. It's not limited to adjusting our diet and hoping for good physical results. It's about recalibrating our souls so that we want to change—spiritually, physically, and mentally." **(Lysa TerKeurst, *Made to Crave: Satisfying Your Deepest Desire with God, Not Food*. Zondervan, 2010, page 16.)**

God is the One who helps us want to change. If you truly desire to change, then you must turn to God for help. Lasting change is not gained by self-effort. Even though the fruit is called "self-control," we only gain this fruit by being connected to our life-source—God.

As we lose our lives to Him, we gain the ability to be our true selves. He is the One who created us. He is the One who has designed us to follow Him.

*"For we are His workmanship, created in Christ Jesus for good works,
which God prepared beforehand that we should walk in them."*
Ephesians 2:10, NKJV

God Himself has designed you with a purpose. He is the Master Designer, and you are His craftsmanship—His masterpiece. He has created you and planned for you specific works. Not only that, but He has prepared beforehand that you would walk in them.

When we give in to self-indulgence, we strip the blueprints from the Master Designer's hands, making changes we desire to appease our need for instant gratification. If we want to achieve the goals of our callings, we must allow God to be in charge. When we embrace Him, the fruit of self-control is able to operate in our lives.

Reflection Questions

1. List the area(s) of self-indulgence that you are tempted to walk in. (Examples are overeating, over-shopping, drugs, alcohol, etc.).

2. Take a moment to reflect on how your overindulgence has impacted your parent-child relationship. Do you overindulge your child with "treats" out of guilt? Does your child tend to overindulge in certain areas?

Group Discussion

What competes with your craving for God? Share an example of when you gave something up in order to follow Jesus more closely.

How can we pray for you?

Study Guide

LESSON 11:

LEARNING TO GIVE LIFE

—⧉—

God is the Life-Giver. He cherishes each life on this planet. No child is a mistake. Every child is precious to Him, for which He has a unique plan.

God is the One who designed motherhood and fatherhood. Since the beginning, it's been His plan to use the family to bring Him glory.

Learning to be a Life-Giving Mom is cooperating with God's redemptive plan for the universe. To redeem is to reclaim someone from bondage. It is to pay the price to save someone from destruction. Jesus is the ultimate Redeemer. He paid the price for the sin of all humanity and gave us the opportunity for a new life in Him.

God's process of redemption begins now. He takes the mess of life and makes it into a message. Often, He uses moms and dads to be messengers of redemption in a child's life. Sometimes that redemption involves paying the cost of adoption.

Mary Beth and Steven Curtis Chapman uniquely understood God's redemptive nature when they first adopted. Mary Beth shares her heart in how it felt when they first adopted Shaohannah.

> God's process of redemption begins now. He takes the mess of life and makes it into a message.

Mary Beth's Story

"Adopting Shaohannah, our first little girl from China, was a big step of faith… I was so afraid. I really felt like 'I'm not going to feel the same. It's not going to be fair.' All of that was just not true.

The minute I laid eyes on her, I would have died for her. God really met me in that hallway in China. As audibly as I could hear Him speak, He spoke the message of the gospel.

'Do you not get it now, you thickheaded woman? Shaohannah didn't do anything to get into your family. She didn't have a name. She didn't have hope. But now she is yours. She has your name. She has your inheritance. She has hope. It's the same thing that I did for you through Jesus.'

I literally heard all of that as I was receiving her. It was as if the world just stopped its motion. From then on my heart was really captured to do more for adoption. I didn't know at that time that meant two more for us." **(Mary Beth Chapman, "Choosing to See" video testimony on SCCchannel YouTube, http://www.youtube.com/watch?v=AgbnjE20vs0.)**

Our children come into our lives without a name and without a hope of surviving without us. They are dependent on us.

In the same way, before the foundation of the earth, God thought of us. As a generous Father, He wanted us to be a part of His family.

> *"God decided in advance to adopt us into his own*
> *family by bringing us to himself through Jesus Christ.*
> *This is what he wanted to do, and it gave him great pleasure."*
> Ephesians 1:5, NLT

The very nature of God is to be a redeemer in your relationships. He is able to go down deep in your heart and life to first heal you, then help to bring about healing in others. When God, our perfect

Father, put His children, Adam and Eve, in a garden of paradise He allowed them to choose (Genesis 1-2). Yet, even when they made a choice that broke relationship with Him, He provided a path of redemption through sending His only Son, Jesus (John 3:16). He laid down His life for you and for your children.

As a mother, you are a nurturing force in your family. As your children make mistakes, point them to the ultimate Redeemer who has paid the price for their sins.

In the same way, I want to remind you that you are first a daughter to God, your Father. Your role as a Life-Giving Mom is secondary to your calling as a daughter.

You may have made mistakes. You could have regrets. It doesn't matter. God will take even your mistakes and make them your message. Joel Osteen says this, "You may have made mistakes but I will tell you: *God's mercy is bigger than any mistake you've made. You may have wasted years of your life making poor choices, but I will tell you God still has a way to carry you to your final destination.*" **(Joel Osteen, *I Declare: 31 Promises to Speak Over Your Life*, FaithWords, 2012, page 90.)**

God's hand is on your back. He's running alongside, encouraging you. You can do it! God has a plan for your life. Part of that plan is being a Life-Giving Mom.

A larger part of God's plan for your life is being His daughter. Enjoy walking hand-in-hand with Him. He is the best father anyone could ever have. You are safe in His presence.

As a father, He has plans for you. He holds the blueprints for your life in His hands. Because He is God, He is able to take the broken pieces of your life and make it part of His master design.

As you hold in your heart the children that He has given you to steward, remember that they are His first. You are partnering in His life plan for their lives.

Reflection Questions

1. What regrets do you have in your role as a mom? What areas do you feel called to change?

2. Consider your part in God's redemptive plan in the lives of your children. How does this impact the way you relate to them when they fail to live up to expectations?

3. Put your own prayer to God in writing, giving Him thanks for all He has done for you.

Group Discussion

Your first role is being a daughter to your Father in heaven. Are you comfortable with that image?

As the group reflects on a parent's role in God's plan of redemption, share what life-giving part you play right now, with your child's specific age.

How can we pray for you?

Additional Resources

Additional Resources
GOING DEEPER
IN FORGIVENESS

If you have bitterness and resentment bubbling in your heart like a toxic swamp, you need to cultivate a lifetime practice of forgiveness. If you don't, the fumes of unforgiveness will poison your thoughts toward others. In a family setting, you may need to forgive one another daily.

Reflections on Forgiveness
- Forgiveness is not forgetting. Only God is able to forget.
- Forgiveness does not mean I must tolerate sin.
- Forgiveness does not seek revenge or demand repayment.
- Forgiveness does mean resolving to live with the consequences of another person's sin.
- Forgiveness is trusting God to bring justice.
- Forgiveness is not a place I "get to," it's the place where I start.
- Forgiveness sets me free from my past.
- Forgiveness is not for the other person's healing, it's for mine.
- Forgiveness allows God to heal my emotional core.
- Forgiveness is God's way of stopping the abuse.
- Forgiveness is how to stop the pain of torment!

Jesus' Words on Forgiveness:
"Our Father in heaven, may your name be kept holy.
May your Kingdom come soon.
May your will be done on earth, as it is in heaven.

*Give us today the food we need, and **forgive us our sins,**
as we have forgiven those who sin against us.
And don't let us yield to temptation, but rescue us from the evil one.*
Matthew 6:9-13 NLT

*"Do not judge others, and you will not be judged.
Do not condemn others, or it will all come back against you.
Forgive others, and you will be forgiven."*
Luke 6:37, NLT

*"I tell you, her sins—and they are many—have been **forgiven**,
so she has shown me much love. But a person who is
forgiven little shows only little love."*
Luke 7:47, NLT

Ask Yourself These Questions:

Whenever our heart is not at peace, it should be a sign to us to look deeper. Here are some questions that you can ask yourself:

- Is there an area in my life where I need to humble myself?
- Do I need to change my heart, attitude, or actions?
- Do I need to admit that I am wrong?
- Is there a "low road" of reconciliation that I am to travel?

Seek to hear God's perspective on the above questions. We can deceive ourselves. Seek God and He will show you steps to take to truly forgive from the heart.

In every relationship, we make our best effort at being genuinely honest in order to walk in healthy relationships. Unresolved relationships bring toxicity into our mental health that seeps into how we relate to our children. Our children can be the innocent bystanders who reap the harvest of unresolved issues in our own lives. The joy of walking with Jesus is that we are able to build a bridge of reconciliation in our hearts and lives. We can live free from offense every day.

Quotes on Forgiveness

"Our Saviour kneels down and gazes upon the darkest acts of our lives. But rather than recoil in horror, he reaches out in kindness and says, 'I can clean that if you want.' And from the basin of his grace, he scoops a palm full of mercy and washes our sin."
—**Max Lucado**

"He that carries bitterness to bed with him will find the devil creeping between the sheets." —**William Secher**

"Forgiveness doesn't make the other person right, it makes you free." —**Stormie Omartian**

"Forgiveness is the key that unlocks the door of resentment and the handcuffs of hatred. It is a power that breaks the chains of bitterness and the shackles of selfishness." —**Corrie Ten Boom**

""Forgiveness is the fragrance the violet sheds on the heel that has crushed it." —**Mark Twain**

"The most miserable prison in the world is the prison we make for ourselves when we refuse to show mercy. Our thoughts become shackled, our emotions are chained, the will is almost paralyzed. But when we show mercy, all of these bonds are broken, and we enter into a joyful liberty that frees us to share God's love with others."
—**Warren W. Wiersbe**

"Those who say they will forgive but can't forget, simply bury the hatchet but leave the handle out for immediate use."
—**Dwight L. Moody**

Choose a quote or a scripture that brings peace, and meditate on it daily. Let it be a healing salve to your wounded heart.

Acknowledgments
9 TRAITS OF A LIFE-GIVING MOM

My heart is filled with deep gratitude.

To my Lover, Jesus: Your love is the most powerful force in my life. Your truth sets me free to be all that I am called to be. Your grace empowers me daily. Your faithfulness endures when things are hard. You know my every need. I want to share Your love and presence with everyone I meet. I have been so transformed by You that I want everyone to know You intimately. The words of this book are my sack lunch offering to You. Just like you used the loaves and fish that the little boy gave to You, I pray that You would take this book, bless it, and multiply it to be shared with the ones who need the message in these pages.

To my husband, Wayne, you are the love of my life. Patient, gentle, and kind, you walk in the fruit of the Spirit every day. Your character and integrity provoke me to be a better person. Our common love and loyalty for Jesus has guided our life and home. Your encouragement strengthens me. Your love surrounds me. We are His workmanship, and He designed us to be side-by-side sharing the good news of His message together. What a joy!

To my parents: Donna, you marked me for ministry while I was still in your womb. You claimed Jeremiah 1:5 in my life: "I knew you before I formed you in your mother's womb. Before you were born I set you apart and appointed you as my prophet to the nations." Allen, you called out my gifts of leadership, ministry, and writing. Before you died you challenged me to write every day.

To my children: My daughters: Rachel Joy, Angela Grace, Hannah Elizabeth, Sarah Faith, you are growing to be women of beauty, grace, and character. Each one of you is so unique, designed and fashioned by God for His purpose and plan. Thank you for the grace you have extended to me as your imperfect mom who loves you so much. My sons, Alexandre Joel and Ezequiel Paul, God planned for you to be our sons. Although I did not hold you in my arms when you were first born, I will hold you in my heart forever. Dustin and Bryan, welcome to the family. You have each chosen your brides well. I look forward to the years ahead.

To my team: Rhonda, what a joy to build a friendship as we work together. Your skill as a writer and editor and the wisdom you bring as a mom of nine… WOW! Lindsay, you are a dream releaser. God uses you to put His message on paper. Sarah, I remember sitting at coffee talking about your book, and you said, "I'm committed to help your voice be heard through print." You are gifted as a writer and designer. You used to be like a daughter; now you are more a friend. Pam, thank you for our long walks together when we first talked about this book. Your friendship has made me a better person. Terry, you pursued me diligently to publish this book. Thank you for your heartfelt commitment to this book and to me as a writer. To David, Margo, and Bethany, and the rest of the Morgan James team, thank you for the opportunity to reach out beyond myself to share this message.

To the women who have shared your stories… Some of you I have met, but most of you have been role models to me as you have written blogs, books, and songs, and shared your stories. You have shared your life transparently. You have walked as life-giving moms who have answered God's call on your lives.

To the body of Christ: Pete Wilson and Cross Point Community Church, your passion about seeking God and sharing Him with others is profoundly transforming. To Glenn Burris and The Foursquare Church, your commitment to mobilize mission inspires me to share the good news to the nations. To Dale Evrist and New Song Christian Fellowship, your love for the Word of God continues to strengthen me every day. To Henry Coles and Faith Life Church, your walk of faith challenges me to believe God for all He has said. To the many pastors, leaders, and intercessors around the world who have taught me and prayed for me, thank you.

About the Author

———✦———

Sue Detweiler's experience in marriage, motherhood, and ministry exemplifies the life of a woman who has embraced her call and is fully alive to all that God has created her to be.

Sue is a gifted teacher, speaker, writer, and leader. As a faithful steward, Sue has developed her God-given talent to communicate and articulate profound truths in simple and relatable ways.

Trial by Fire

As a young mom, Sue Detweiler nearly lost her 5-week-old baby when she awoke to find her house on fire. By God's grace she and her baby were rescued, but afterwards she felt as if her whole life was "on fire" as she struggled to rebuild her house and home.

"A breakthrough in my life took place when I realized that I couldn't do anything apart from God. Staying connected to the life-giving strength of Jesus Christ is the only way I can parent my children and be an encouragement to others. I was already an ordained minister pastoring a church with my husband, but being saved from the fire gave me a heart to help save others going through 'fires' in their lives."

Approaching her 30th birthday in 1993, she felt led by God to launch a radio program to encourage other young mothers who shared her struggles. Feeling like she was not an expert at being a mom, she obeyed anyway and launched a syndicated radio feature called "Harmony at Home."

Putting it All on the Altar, Again and Again

As the ministry began to grow, she had an opportunity to expand her outreach to television. She had four children under 7 and, after much prayer, felt God was calling her to put all of her energy into His number one priority—her family. So, like Abraham, she put her media ministry on the altar, pouring her life into her husband, children, and local church. While homeschooling her young family, she became the principal of New Song Christian Academy where her children were enrolled; oversaw LIFE School of Ministry, an award-winning Bible Training Institute for pastors and leaders; taught Bible and Theology; and served as an Associate Pastor at New Song Christian Fellowship.

In 2007, just when it seemed like things were finally settling down with their children moving into their older teenage years, God began to call Wayne and Sue to open their hearts to adoption. Sue heard the Lord say, "Well done, but I have more children for you."

Once again, they laid everything on the altar and adopted two young orphan boys from Brazil. Unaware of the emotional and learning challenges they would face, Sue and Wayne quickly became intimately aware of the day-to-day struggles of helping "orphans" become sons.

A Deeper Message, a Broader Ministry

Called by God to bring healing and redemption, God is now calling Sue to take the depth of life experience He has given her as a result of her obedience and share it with everyone through books, radio, video, writing, and speaking. Sue is an inspiration and a voice of stability, offering men and women practical help from a biblical perspective.

If you would like to invite Sue to speak at your event or follow her blog, visit **www.SueDetweiler.com**.

LIFE COACHING

with

WAYNE & SUE DETWEILER

Do you desire to grow into your God-given callings? Life Coaching is for you! You will be amazed at how your life can experience dramatic change as you walk with a Life Coach.

A few months of coaching can transform the way you live the rest of your life as a husband, wife, mother, father, businessman, or working mom. Concentrate on what you truly value in life.

As your coaches, we can help you achieve your highest potential by identifying your gifts, overcoming obstacles, and clarifying your vision.

Our times of connecting are done over the telephone or internet so it is convenient to your schedule. Simply contact wayne@life-bridges.org to set up your free 15-minute consultation.

Go to **Life-Bridges.com** or **SueDetweiler.com** for more information on Coaching Packages, FREE Resources, or booking a speaking event.

CPSIA information can be obtained at www.ICGtesting.com
Printed in the USA
LVOW07s1342160115

423137LV00009B/174/P